Intimacy and Awe

Walking with the Real God

Herb Shaffer

Velvet Mallet Publishing
Pittsburgh, Pennsylvania

We want to hear from you!
Please send your comments to herbshaffer@hotmail.com or 4767 Library Road, Bethel Park, PA 15102

Intimacy and Awe: Walking With the Real God
Copyright © 2018 by Herb Shaffer. All rights reserved.

Permission Notice:
Portions of this book may be quoted (in written, visual, audio, or electronic form) for not-for-profit purposes without express written permission of the author if credit is given and quotation does not exceed ten pages.

Portions of this book may not be reproduced for-profit without the express written permission of the author, with the exception of brief quotations.

Printed in the United States of America

First Printing, 2018

Velvet Mallet Publishing

All scripture quotations, unless otherwise indicated, are taken from *The ESV Bible* (Holy Bible, English Standard Version): 2011. Wheaton, IL: Crossway, a publishing ministry of Good News Publishers. Used by permission. All rights reserved.

Scriptures marked NIV are taken from *The Holy Bible: New International Version*. 1984. Grand Rapids, MI: Zondervan.

Scriptures marked NLT are taken from *The New Living Translation*, Tyndale House Publishers. (2007). *Holy Bible: New Living Translation* (3rd ed.) Carol Stream, IL: Tyndale House Publishers

Scriptures marked MSG are taken from *The Message*, Peterson, E. H. (2005). *The Message: The Bible in contemporary language*. Colorado Springs, CO: NavPress.

Scriptures marked NRSV are taken from *The Holy Bible: New Revised Standard Version*. 1989. Nashville: Thomas Nelson Publishers.

Credits
Editorial review by Kelly Opferman
Cover design by Amber Bethel
Cover photograph by Michael Matti, www.michaelmatti.com

The Christian does not think God will love us because we are good, but that God will make us good because He loves us.
— C.S. Lewis[1]

Being a Christian is more than just an instantaneous conversion. It is a daily process whereby you grow to be more and more like Christ. — Billy Graham[2]

Intimacy

You make known to me the path of life; you will fill me with joy in your presence, with eternal pleasures at your right hand.
-- Psalm 16:11

This resurrection life you received from God is not a timid, grave-tending life. It's adventurously expectant, greeting God with a childlike 'What's next, Papa?'
-- Romans 8:15 (The Message)

Awe

Then Joshua told the people: 'You can't do it; you're not able to worship God. He is a holy God. He is a jealous God. He won't put up with your fooling around and sinning.'
-- Joshua 24:19 (The Message)

Holy, holy, holy Is God our Master, Sovereign-Strong, The Was, The Is, The Coming.
-- Revelation 4:8b (The Message)

---

[1] Lewis, C.S. (1952). *Mere Christianity*. New York: MacMillan.
[2] "A Daily Process" devotion series, © 2018 Billy Graham Evangelistic Assn.

CONTENTS

Introduction: A New Way of Seeing 1

PART ONE: Knowing God For Real

1. An Invitation I Tried to Refuse 6
2. Valuing the Valuable 10
3. Walking to Your Own Funeral 12
4. God in Your Pocket 14
5. The Haircut 16

PART TWO: The True View of God

6. What's in Your Wallet? 20
7. The Right Picture of God 26
8. Letting Jesus Be God-Sized 33
9. Pigs in a Blanket 37

PART THREE: When Jesus Shows Up

10. Amazing Things Happen When Jesus Shows Up 40
11. When God is Working Most 44
12. The Very, Very Best and Worst Day of All 47
13. Jesus Was Always Picking Fights 50

PART FOUR: Holy and Holding

14. Can God Be Both Power and Love? 54
15. Is God Really There? 58
16. Jaw-Dropping Grace 61
17. What is God Feeling? 64
18. Charley and the NIS 67

PART FIVE: "On" is Way Different Than "With"

19. Not Just "With" God 76
20. "Merry" or "Mighty" Christmas? 80
21. I Know Your Hurt 83
22. Sometimes You Need Someone 85

PART SIX: We Lost It All and Need It Back

23. The Enormity of What We Lost 90
24. I Want My Heart Back! 93
25. What Did We Expect? 97
26. Don't Feed the Animal 100
27. When Tragedy Strikes, Do This First 102

PART SEVEN: Don't Just Sit There

28. The First of Many Steps 106
29. Living for the Dot or the Line 110
30. You Might Be Selfish If 112
31. Worthship That is True 115
32. Storms 119

PART EIGHT: Never Ending, Ever Changing

33. It's the Start 124
34. There Just Aren't Enough Hugs 129
35. God and I Had a Fight 132
36. When Jesus Was Strongest 136

Epilogue

The Joy We Get, The Joy We Give 140
About the Author 145
Bibliography/Footnotes 147

INTRODUCTION

A NEW WAY OF SEEING

Can You See It?

"Dad, Dad! Look at this!" said my oldest son, Andrew, as he walked into the living room with an open book in his hand. "This is so cool!" he said, pointing to a multi-colored graphic of...nothing. To me, it was a bunch of colored shapes. Nice colors, mind you, but I didn't get his excitement. Ordinarily, this middle-schooler was impressed with nothing short of shaking hands with a professional baseball player or landing on the moon. I felt his forehead for the fever that would explain enthusiasm for a book of colored shapes.

"There's nothing there," I said confidently. He smiled. I know that smile. So do you. It's the one that communicates with a simple facial expression that he knows something that his dad doesn't, therefore he is highly intelligent and his dad is a cave man (with all due respect to cave men).

"Yes, there is, Dad. The picture is hidden."

I looked again. More closely. Stared and searched, grasping to regain my "dad is smart" standing. Not. A. Thing. And the boy once again smiled that condescending smile.

"There is nothing there," I said, with what I hoped was confidence. "You're just trying to fool me."

"No, really, Dad. Look at the picture. There are dinosaurs."

"Sheila, what is the doctor's number? We need to take this boy there quick. He's hallucinating."

"Daaaad!" he said, using the universal pronunciation children use when frustrated and disgusted. Especially when the man who sired them tells "dad" jokes.

"You have to look *through* the picture to see the hidden picture. It's a 'Magic Eye'[1] picture."

I made for the car keys thinking we should go to straight to the ER and bypass the doctor.

"Just try it, Dad." I tried it. Nothing. Except the mish-mash of colors as before.

The smile turned to delighted, patronizing laughter.

"I can see it," a voice sounded. I glanced up to see my daughter peering over my shoulder. "There are four dinosaurs. Two in the back, one there and a baby in the front. Aww, isn't he cute?!"

"You guys are just messing with me. How long have you been concocting this? You're all grounded."

"I don't go anywhere, Dad. How can you ground me?" said the little female at my side.

"Here, Dad. Let me show you," Andrew said, appearing to be helpful. I couldn't help but wonder what the next act in the humiliation play would be.

"Hold the book up to your nose, keep your eyes the way they are now and slowly move the picture away from you."

Right.

But I dutifully did it expecting raucous laughter at any moment as these hooligans pulled something on me.

"OH! Right. RIGHT!" I exclaimed in amazement, the dinosaurs coming more and more clearly into focus.

"See! SEE! I told you!"

"You were right, I conceded. I saw it all along. I was just pulling your leg."

"Daaaaaaad!"

But he was right. I didn't see the dinosaurs at first, though they were always there. Not until I learned a new way of seeing could I make out the depth of what was there, the real beauty in the picture.

A New Way of Seeing and Knowing God

The problem was not that the dinosaurs were missing, or that the design of the picture was wrong, or that I wasn't trying, or even that my eyes were not working. The problem was with the way I was looking. To see the Magic Eye picture for what it really was necessitated a new way of seeing; the ability to look past the superficial to see the real picture. I couldn't do it by myself, though. This new way of seeing required a guide who had experienced it to show me the way. As a result and to my delight, I saw what had been there all along.

I believe that many people are looking for God, but not seeing Him. The problem is not that God is hiding from us, but that we need a new ways of seeing. Ever since the Garden of Eden debacle, men and women have struggled to see God as He really is. Sometimes hidden, sometimes distorted, sometimes defaced, the true picture of God calls to us just beyond the superficial. As a result, we are hindered from experiencing a true relationship with God. A relationship that satisfies the longing in our hearts, fills the hole in our souls, makes sense out of life, provides us purpose and gives us hope.

My hope is that this book will lead you to a new way of seeing and thus a new way of experiencing the relationship with God you have always longed for. That it will guide you to see past the superficial to what is really real with God. That, through this book, you will allow me to be your guide to a relationship with God of intimacy and awe. Not because I have it all figured out, but because I might be a few steps farther down the path.

> 'You will seek me and find me, when you seek me with all your heart. I will be found by you,' declares the Lord,
> -- Jeremiah 29:13–14a

> 'For my thoughts are not your thoughts, neither are your ways my ways,' declares the Lord. 'As the heavens are higher than the earth, so are my ways higher than your ways and my thoughts than your thoughts.'   -- Isaiah 55:8–9

> 'Call to me and I will answer you and tell you great and unsearchable things you do not know.'
> -- Jeremiah 33:3

PART ONE

Knowing God For REAL!

Part One: Knowing God for Real

CHAPTER ONE

AN INVITATION I TRIED TO REFUSE

When your loving Heavenly Dad invites you to do something that you long for, but scares you silly, what do you do?

"Come sit on my lap."

Those were the words that began to wreck my heart and my life.

Those were words that I never expected to hear. Not anywhere on the fringes of my radar. And yet, there they were.

It was the fall of 1998 when it happened. One of my best friends, Jim Harvey, told me about fasting and modeled very practical ways to use it to connect with God. As I gave in to Jim's badgering, I discovered he was right. I built regular fasting into my schedule. But I never, ever expected anything like this.

"Come sit on my lap."

During one of the three day juice fasts, while praying at my desk, a picture came to mind. A picture and words from God. Now before you remark, "Oh, Herb is one of *those*," please understand that I'm not claiming to see apocalyptic visions or that I go into supernatural trances. But it does seem that, when God wants to show me something important, He does it by bringing pictures and words to mind. Out of the ordinary pictures and words that dive through my mind and heart to land in my soul.

"Come sit on my lap."

Those were the inaudible words I sensed as a picture of God sitting on a throne came into my mind. I was ready for God to give me any instruction. Actually, correction is what I most expected. For Him to tell me where I was going wrong or that I needed to shape up in some way. I was ready for instructions on being a better husband, parent or pastor. I would not have been surprised to hear directions for the church or even to pick up the family and move. There was nothing that would have surprised me except…an invitation to experience this level of familiarity with God.

"Come sit on my lap."

There are very few times when it is appropriate to sit on a person's lap. Only two that I can think of. A wife with her husband. A child with a trusted family member, most often a parent. Sitting on another's lap is so very, very, very intimate. It is an experience of closeness, of a familiarity shared by few. Putting God in the same sentence with intimacy was not in my repertoire. I thought of God in a lot of ways, but I never imagined crawling into His holy lap.

"Come sit on my lap."

My relationship with my human father was troubled at best. Marked by the emotional abuse of words that consistently body slammed me to the ground, distant would be a kind description of our relationship. I grew up longing for life-giving verbal and physical affirmation, but received scraps. I walled my heart off from closeness out of pure protection and survival. In 1998, twenty-three years removed from daily living in that emotional morass, God gave me an invitation that would rock my world.

"Come sit on my lap."

I shake my head when I realize that I had been a Christian for over 25 years and a pastor for more than 15 years. I had taught, preached, counseled and written about relationship with God. I was confident I knew what it meant. Turns out I knew *about* God, but I only superficially *knew* God. I was reeling as those words kept echoing through the cavern of my soul.

"Come sit on my lap."

Being the spiritual pastor that I am, I responded as God knew I would. *"I CAN'T!!"* I cried out. "I want to, but I can't!"

Yeah, I know. Not what you were expecting. It was the only honest response. When God shows up so clearly, it's prudent to be honest.

It wasn't that I didn't *want* to. It's that I could not bring myself to believe that God could want me to come that close. When you've been stung a hundred times, you stay far away from the bee hive. Even though it was not God who stung me, I could not bring myself to obey. I was spiritually paralyzed. It ended there and the picture was gone.

Except when it wasn't. That was every time I prayed. The picture and the words re-emerged every time I prayed. The conversation and the scene played out the same every time. For SIX MONTHS. God is persistent when He wants His way, when He wants us to have what is best for us,

Part One: Knowing God for Real

when He wants to heal our souls, and when He sees we are the hurting, helpless, pitiful children that we are. I am inexpressibly grateful that God is the "hound of Heaven" who relentlessly pursues.

One day, after half a year, God and I were at it again.

"Come sit on my lap," He said.

"I CAN'T, but I want to!" I replied.

Then, for some reason I added, "If you will help me, I will."

Everything changed! That was all it took. The picture of God on the throne changed. One moment, it was the familiar scene of Him sitting with open arms of invitation. The next moment, the picture transformed to God reaching down to me, picking me up, sitting me on His lap and wrapping His arms around me. And I began to bawl. I could feel His arms around me, flooding me with feelings of value I had never experienced before.

Something significant changed in me that day. Chains were broken. Walls fell. Distance was breeched. And I have never been the same.

"Come sit on my lap," has become a welcome invitation every time I pray. I can close my eyes and sense myself being pulled onto God's lap. I tear up every time it happens in response to the overwhelming intimacy of God's love and His unrelenting pursuit of this close and personal relationship with me.

Intimacy.

Another Description of Intimacy

Intimacy is the word that captures the description of God's care expressed in the Old Testament book of Zephaniah:

> The Lord your God is in your midst, a mighty one who will save; he will rejoice over you with gladness; he will quiet you by his love; he will exult over you with loud singing.
> -- Zephaniah 3:17

This is a picture of a strong, loving daddy holding a small child who is upset, perhaps scared, in pain, or over tired. Thrilled to have the child in his arms, he quiets the little one with words and touches of love. Later, the child awakes to find daddy singing loudly as he picks the child up with

Lord, I want an intimacy that stirs my emotions to ecstasy

great joy. A treasured, cherished child and a strong, loving Dad experiencing an intimate relationship.

Look at Zephaniah's words:

"in your midst"—God is right with us.

"a mighty one who will save"—Powerful, God will protect and rescue.

"rejoice over you with gladness"—Great joy to have us in His arms. Great gladness just because we are together.

"he will quiet you by his love"—He will settle us, love on us, let us know it will be okay.

"he will exult over you with loud singing."—God sings over us with great delight.

The Invitation is for You!

God did not invite me to sit on His lap because I deserved it, earned it or was more valuable than anyone else. It was because God is love and created us for intimacy with Him. All of us. That means God is inviting you as well.

Accept that invitation in whatever forms it arrives. And as quickly as you can.

Perhaps this moment is your invitation. As you read my story, maybe you felt the same tug to climb on to God's lap. If so, put the book down and do it. You can't imagine how thrilled God will be or the joy filled satisfaction that will overflow your soul.

> However, those the Father has given me will come to me, and I will never reject them. -- John 6:37 (NLT)

> Come to me, all who labor and are heavy laden, and I will give you rest. Take my yoke upon you, and learn from me, for I am gentle and lowly in heart, and you will find rest for your souls. For my yoke is easy, and my burden is light."
> -- Matthew 11:28–30

CHAPTER TWO

VALUING THE VALUABLE

To sit on God's lap means we learn to value what He values by being with our loving Heavenly Dad.

I looked around after walking and walking and walking. I was in the same place. How could this be? I had to be making progress. The sweat pouring out of my body told me so. The ache in my muscles could not have been for nothing, could it? But it was excruciatingly obvious I was in the same spot from which I started at least forty-five minutes and two miles ago. Same scenery, same building, same place. In spite of great effort, I had made no progress at all. Then I stepped off the treadmill. In my basement.

Yeah. I know.

Actually, I did make progress because my purpose was not to get anywhere, but to get exercise. In fact, it was surprisingly worthwhile because I prayed and read a great book while I walked. If I had been trying to get to a specific, physical destination, the treadmill was wrong. When we want to cover ground, we need to step off the treadmill to solid ground.

Our dog hasn't been for a walk in a while. She loves going for jaunts. She covers twice as much ground as we do, back and forth, back and forth sniffing out varmints. I thought about putting her on the treadmill for exercise. She's looking pretty lethargic. I explained to Sheila, "Just put her on slow and let her walk. As she gets used to it, we can speed it up ... and see what happens." I thought I was being helpful. Well, sure, a misstep might throw her into the washing machine but hey, no pain, no gain. Sheila wasn't amused.

If you're like many people I see these days, you're on a treadmill, too. Different from the one in my basement, but just as draining. It's called life. Instead of having joy, peace, meaning, love, and feeling alive as we walk, it seems we are doing everything we can to just keep trudging, one foot after another, simply so we don't get thrown off the treadmill.

Does anyone believe this is an accident? That the Lord who came and lived in a body just like ours, would give us a life that feels like a treadmill to nowhere? A life that wears us out and leaves us spent? Or could it be a carefully designed strategy to cause us to miss that which is of utmost value? Think about it – if you hatched a plan to derail people from experiencing "God with us," what would you do? Wouldn't you distract, disrupt, hurry, overwhelm, and appeal to their selfishness?

Immediately below our relationship with God, what is most important? People. But what do the pressures of our culture cause us to zero in on? Material possessions and activity. Who made it a rule that we have to spend money that we don't have, to do things that will wear us out and strain relationships with people we love? Who said that pursuing the things and activities of life has to consume us? How many times have we gotten upset with the very people we say we love because stuff didn't go the way we thought it should go? Sure, we all have things we have to do, but does it really have to be like this? I have a suggestion.

For three weeks, let's create a conspiracy to value the really valuable – relationship with God and relationship with the people in our lives. Slow down, eliminate some activity, decrease the focus on material stuff and deeply enjoy God's purpose for our lives: God and people.

Take time to sit with God, read the Bible, listen to uplifting music (better yet, sing along), and do those things that allow God to refresh us.

Make time to be with, not just occupy the same general area, but *really be with* family and friends. Let some of the activity go. Pause to realize how fragile life is and live what matters with purpose. Refuse to take people for granted, realizing they won't always be with us. Do whatever it takes to value our loved ones; and **tell them!**

Let's step off the treadmill and on to God's real life.

> Show me, O LORD, my life's end and the number of my days; let me know how fleeting is my life. You have made my days a mere handbreadth; the span of my years is as nothing before you. Each man's life is but a breath. -- Psalm 39:4-5

> And now these three remain: faith, hope and love. But the greatest of these is love. -- 1 Corinthians 13:13

Part One: Knowing God for Real

CHAPTER THREE

WALKING TO YOUR OWN FUNERAL

To sit on God's lap leads us to live truly alive

Imagine you get the dreaded phone call – your son/brother has been killed in an auto accident. Grief overwhelms you. Relatives go to the morgue to identify the body, glance, turn away, horrified at the brutal injuries, but acknowledge it is the missing family member.

The funeral is scheduled for the next day on "The Day of the Dead," a holiday when loved ones who have died the previous year are honored.

Before the memorial service begins, you stand in front of the casket, tears streaming down your face, thinking, "What a waste! We didn't even get to say good-bye." As you mourn, looking at the body, arm in arm with your closest loved ones, you look up toward the door to spot a man walking purposefully toward you. You blink, look at the body, look at the man, look at the corpse, look at the man, look at the dead, look at the man walking toward you – it is your son/brother! Some people gasp, some faint, some jump out of the windows as the man you identified in the morgue continues to walk toward you.

"This does not happen!" you cry. "Dead people do not walk around."

And yet, here he is walking to his own funeral. It's enough to cause some of the people in the room to need their own funeral.

Amazingly, I did not make this up. It happened to Ademir Jorge Goncalves, a bricklayer from Brazil, and his family.

Not only was it a shock for his family, it was disconcerting for him when, upon arriving home, a shaken relative told him that everyone was gone to a funeral and the funeral was for him. Turns out his family had mistakenly identified the body of a victim of a car accident as Goncalves.

Gives a whole new meaning to the phrase "dead man walking."

Dead people don't walk. Or do they?

Depends on your definition of "dead."

"Dead" means not alive, not functioning as living, the life has left the body, it has ceased to fulfill its purpose.

You don't have to go to a funeral home to see dead people. They are walking all around us every day. They appear to be alive, but life has drained from them and they are perfunctorily going through the motions. For some, life's weariness has sucked all enthusiasm and purpose from them. For others, tragedy was too much and robbed them of life. For others, it was betrayal. In each case, hope was removed and with it the ability to be alive. You can watch them walk, but look into their eyes and no one's home.

That's what happens when hope is gone. Even worse, the problem with having no hope is that you cannot conjure even a spark of hope that there will ever be hope again.

Dead people walking. It could be us. Maybe you are one of them. Hearts are beating, lungs are drawing air several times a minute, but they are meandering without life. They go through the motions but have lost purpose, joy, meaning, fulfillment, *life*! Sometimes they are hard to spot because there are so many of them around. Other times, you can see the glazed look and apathy. Maybe you see it when you brush your teeth. The walking dead settle for things that temporarily provide pleasure and then return to living graves.

But Jesus offers more. His heart breaks for those who should be alive but are not. Jesus came to bring people back to life. Jesus died to bring people back to life. Jesus came back to life to bring people back to life. Jesus now sits at the right hand of the Father praying for people to come back to life. Jesus said,

'Because I live, you also will live.' -- John 14:19b

'I came so they can have real and eternal life, more and better life than they ever dreamed of.' -- John 10:10 (The Message)

If you are one of the walking dead, crawl up on God's lap and let Him restore your life. Just sit and He will do the rest.

Don't walk to your own funeral. Choose life. Every day.

But God, being rich in mercy, because of the great love with which he loved us, even when we were dead in our trespasses, made us alive together with Christ—by grace you have been saved— -- Ephesians 2:4–5

CHAPTER FOUR

GOD IN YOUR POCKET

To sit on God's lap means we let go of old gods to let Him be God

What would you think of a man who carried his god around in his pocket, pulling him out to bow down or talk to him at various times? The pocket god never talked back, never gave direction, never acted like you'd expect a god to act. You'd probably give him plenty of room. "I mean, really," you'd say to me, "How can that thing be god if he can carry him around in his pocket?"

You would be very, very correct. We wouldn't do that…would we?

Truth is we *do* carry around our gods in pockets and purses and don't even realize it. When we define "god" as whatever rules our lives, we do. Be honest. Don't you find that the things that tend to rule our lives are held in our hands or, if too big to physically hold, they possess our minds? God spoke through the prophet Isaiah about this.

> To whom will you compare me? Who is my equal? Some people pour out their silver and gold and hire a craftsman to make a god from it. Then they bow down and worship it! They carry it around on their shoulders, and when they set it down, it stays there. It cannot even move! And when someone prays to it, there is no answer. It has no power to get anyone out of trouble.
> -- Isaiah 46:5 - 7 (NLT)

So what's the job description for god? What does the résumé require? And what disqualifies something from being god?
- ✓ If you can contain it, it is not god.
- ✓ If you can understand it, it is not god.
- ✓ If you can create it, it is not god.
- ✓ If you can control it, it is not god.
- ✓ If you cannot depend on it, it is not god.
- ✓ If it changes, it is not god.

Narrows the list – are we following these disqualifiers? We may not literally bow down to modern "gods" but they rule our lives. Let's apply the above tests to come common gods.

Money is god to many. Can we understand, create, control, or contain it? Can we depend on it? Does it change? Money scores a six out of six, so it fails to qualify as god. And yet, it rules much of the world.

Power is a god to many. Fails.
Popularity/approval is a god to many. Fails.
Success is a god to many. Fails.
Beauty is a god to many. Fails.
Pleasure is a god to many. Fails.
None qualify.

Let's do the same with Jesus. Can we understand Him? Not a chance. Can we create Him? No, He created us. Can we control Him? HA! Much as we think we'd like to at times, we can't. People couldn't even keep Him in line when He walked here. Can we contain Him? The entire universe could not. Can we depend on Him to be there for us, true to His promises? Absolutely. Does He change? His character, personality, and purposes never, ever change. JESUS PASSES! He is the *only* One who can pass to qualify as the real and only God.

That being true, don't you think it a good idea for us to stop acting like what we carry around is god and allow the only true God carry us instead?

> Formerly, when you did not know God, you were enslaved to those that by nature are not gods. -- Galatians 4:8

> For there is one God, and there is one mediator between God and men, the man Christ Jesus, -- 1 Timothy 2:5

> to the only God, our Savior, through Jesus Christ our Lord, be glory, majesty, dominion, and authority, before all time and now and forever. Amen. -- Jude 25

Part One: Knowing God for Real

CHAPTER FIVE

THE HAIRCUT

To sit on God's lap is to trust Him when you head into experiences that are new and frightening

There's a first time for everything, but there is *only* a first time for everything. Every time after is not the first time. And the first time can be momentous. Ask any parent with one child. First step, first tooth, first word, first laugh, first smile. They are precious memories you want to capture. So thousands of pictures are snapped. The second child has the same firsts, but it is not the first for the parent. It is still precious, but you're so busy chasing the first child who is having his first sibling rivalry jealousy fit that you only get a few hundred pictures. The third child, well...somebody posted a photo on Facebook while you were corralling child one and two, right?

It was time for our first grandchild's first haircut. His mother, Carissa, knew it had to be done, but life was busy so the hair got stragglier. Probably some hesitancy on her part to trim those locks as well – there's only one first cutting of that soft baby hair. There's also the fact that Brodie is all boy, all the time, with the energy and curiosity to supply an entire pre-school. So underneath all else was the question of getting him still long enough to use scissors close to the boy's face. Would he lose an ear for the sake of a haircut? Would the stylist lose a finger as Brodie wiggled and wriggled?

But it was time for the first time. At sixteen months, the first grandchild was walking into his first hair salon with Mom, Grandma (equipped camera and twenty-seven multi-gigabyte camera cards) and Grandpa assigned to distract-the-boy during haircut duty. With visions of leaving with half a haircut traipsing through the adults' heads, the four approached the shop.

It was time. Immediately, Brodie broke from Grandpa's hand toward the toys in the waiting area. Rapidly emptying the basket, he moved from toy to toy to toy. Energy to spare. I confess to having little faith about this endeavor. Carissa talked with Anita, the lucky stylist, about this first haircut and how it would play out.

"Oh, yes, we do lots of children's hair. We've had tough ones and we can handle them," said Anita with amazing calm.

"But you've not seen this boy at full tilt," I thought, but did not say aloud. Let me clarify – Brodie is a great kid. He is nice to other kids and dogs, full of laughter and fun. He does not *intentionally* destroy things or get into trouble. It's just that he is so smart, so curious and so full of energy that the constant motion can cause problems. It was that motion and haircut in the same sentence that concerned me. I looked around for a First Aid kit. Maybe for Brodie, maybe for Anita.

Since the first mention of a haircut for the boy weeks before, I simply could not come up with any scenario in which Brodie sat long enough for a few snips, let alone a full haircut. I could not imagine any script for this working out well. What I did imagine was Brodie turning his head with each snip, pushing the cape away because it felt strange, and squirming from the chair. And us leaving with half a haircut and a stylist giving up the profession.

Stylist Anita gave Carissa confidence in the short few minutes that Brodie went through the basket of toys as Grandpa said, "Don't throw that… don't put that in your mouth… let's read the book… okay, let's throw the book…"

"Bring him over to the chair," said stylist Anita. So I did.

"Let's put Mom on the styling chair first," she said as she held out a plastic cape for Carissa. Carissa sat and was fitted with the covering.

"Now let's put Brodie on Mom's lap." I sat him there and Anita wrapped a smaller cape around the child.

"Grandpa, bring that basket over here and let Brodie pick out a lollipop." I did. He chose green apple. Another first, by the way. His first sucker. Which was fortunate for all. Because he didn't quite know what to do with it, the lollipop captured his full attention and all his energy. His effort was part licking, part sucking, part gnawing and a great deal of drooling. (That's what that plastic apron was for!)

And the boy sat still as a statue. Every once in a while, he sputtered when hair hit the sucker, but other than that the toddler was perfect. With full comfort and security on Mom's lap, Brodie was free to put his full concentration on the sweet treat, oblivious to scissors and comb.

Anita is a genius! And the boy looked great!

Anita's genius was in putting Brodie on Mom's lap. Everything else helped, but without the lap nothing else would have worked. There is no place better for a child than the lap when facing new or fearful situations. It provides comfort, security, safety, courage and more. You can accomplish a great deal with a child when he is on a loving parent's lap.

And so it is with God. When God originally invited me onto His lap, it was to break down walls and deepen the relationship He offered. But, I've discovered over the years, there are a lot of reasons to climb onto God's lap. At the top of the list are the times when we are frightened by what is happening, what is new, what is uncertain. The haircut was for Brodie's benefit, but it would not have felt that way without Carissa's lap.

God will do the same with us. Sometimes the frightening things in our lives are for our good, so we are open to what God wants to do and who He really is. God can accomplish a great deal with us, His children, when we are on His lap.

Brodie's haircut was smooth because he didn't fight his mother's lap; he leaned into it and had a great first haircut. When facing the firsts in life, the best place to start is on God's lap. Don't fight it; lean into it. Loving Heavenly Dad's lap is the place to be.

> Come to me, all who labor and are heavy laden, and I will give you rest. Take my yoke upon you, and learn from me, for I am gentle and lowly in heart, and you will find rest for your souls. For my yoke is easy, and my burden is light."
> -- Matthew 11:28–30

PART TWO

The True View of God

Part Two: The True View of God

CHAPTER SIX

WHAT'S IN YOUR WALLET®?

To sit on God's lap requires that we <u>let go of the wrong pictures of God that clutter and clog our minds, hearts</u> and souls

What pictures do you have in your wallet, in your purse or on your phone? Let me rephrase that because some of us have hundreds. Which pictures do you look at or show people most often?

I used to make fun of grandparents. An adult can be a perfectly sane person for decades, but the moment one of their children has a child a crazy grandparent switch flips in the brain and sanity is abandoned. Take a chair if you dare to ask about their grandkids. They will set up a projector to show you the last five hundred pictures taken of this perfect child. And those are just from the past week. I still make fun, but I've joined the fraternity. Even when, as a non-grandparent, I poked fun at grandparents, I knew I would be just like them. It could be why people dodge behind doors and jump into closets when they see me coming. "No more pictures of babies doing adorable things," I hear them cry as I chase them down the street. "Just one more," I yell, waving my phone.

Why are the latest pictures of Brodie, Cadence and Maddie the ones I look at and force on others? Because those are the people I value most.

Standing with a friend, I saw a family picture in his wallet. "Good looking family," I complimented. "Oh, that's not my family. The picture came with the wallet." That boy needs help. Normal people don't keep pictures of strangers in their wallets or leave the sample photos in picture frames. Because we value the picture of people we love.

We could do an Internet search for "best looking kids," print them and put them on our desks or wall. They might be more model beautiful than our own families, but we wouldn't do that. Because we value pictures of people we love, not photogenic strangers.

Nor do we carry pictures of kids when they are at their worst, acting in ways that make us angry, disappointed, and ashamed. I have no pictures of grandkids in the throes of a nasty diaper change or screaming with colic.

Intimacy and Awe: Walking with the Real God

No, we carry pictures that capture good memories, make us feel warm inside, touch us and remind us of the people we love.

What kind of pictures of God do you carry in the wallet of your heart, mind and soul?

What Comes to Mind?

Pause for a moment. Please. Take some time for the following exercise. You may just have an "aha!" moment.

Here it is: stop for a short prayer. Bow your head, close your eyes, and start with, "Dear God…" Go ahead, I'll wait.

When you started to pray, what came to mind? Who are you praying to? What is He like? What is the picture, the image, or the person that came to your mind?

Write it down here: *God pulling me up on his lap and saying, "I'm proud of you. You did what I asked." Wonderful, close feeling*

That picture gives you a good indication of who you believe God to be.[2] What does this image tell you about your view of God? Write that down, too: *The Almighty I want to please.*

"What comes to our minds when we think about God is the most important thing about us." [3]

So says A.W. Tozer, a powerful man of God and deeply spiritual pastor and writer of the 20th century.

The first time I read that quote I was taken aback. Really? *The* most important thing? After chewing on it awhile I realized Tozer is absolutely, completely, 100% correct. Our picture of God is the lens through which we see everything. The photograph of God in our heads determines how we think, feel and act. Even when we are not intentionally taking God into account, the lens subconsciously interprets everything.

E-V-E-R-Y-T-H-I-N-G!

Thus, it just makes sense that we get serious about getting a right view of God.

Why was it so difficult for me to accept God's invitation to sit on His lap? There are factors that, at first glance, seem to be the reasons, such as the childhood experiences with my dad or insufficient Bible teaching. Those contribute but are not the root issue that became the dictator in my soul. My difficulty and attempted refusal was a natural consequence of who I believed God to be.

There are many paths that will take us to the wrong view of God. My path included harsh experiences with my dad and bad information from various sources. Your path may be similar or far different. It doesn't really matter which path we take, the destination is the same – we end up with a wrong view of God. We see God as someone He is not, which, without exception, wreaks havoc in our thoughts, feelings, actions, relationships, choices, and literally everything else. What a mess!

The Wrong View of God

As the Apostle Paul traveled from place to place with the Good News of Jesus, he game to Athens where men gathered in a large plaza to debate and discuss the philosophies of the day. They were religious men who wanted to make sure they worshipped all gods, so idols were prominently placed around the plaza. They were sincerely religious men, but it is possible to be sincere and sincerely wrong. And they were.

> So Paul, standing in the midst of the Areopagus, said: "Men of Athens, I perceive that in every way you are very religious. For as I passed along and observed the objects of your worship, I found also an altar with this inscription: 'To the unknown god.' What therefore you worship as unknown, this I proclaim to you.
> -- Acts 17:22–23

The apostle Paul did not criticize these men, recognizing that *everyone* ends up with wrong views of God. In the beginning, Adam and Eve saw, knew and lived with God as He really is. It was automatic, without effort. It was their nature. When the first couple disobeyed God, bringing sin into the world, a great distortion cloud descended, entering their hearts, minds, souls and bodies. Instead of seeing clearly and living unashamed, they hid from God and one another and could no longer see *anything* clearly. Every person since has a built-in distortion filter that blurs hearts, minds, souls and bodies. It is no longer the natural state to see God as He *really* is.

Thus, one of the worst consequences of sin is that the automatic picture we have of God is incorrect. The good news is that God offers to help us see Him for who He actually is as we work hard to correct our skewed image.

Popular Mistaken Pictures of God

Let's start by digging up our current views of God. Here are some popular versions:

✓ God as a Santa Claus. A big, jolly, kind, teddy bear of a man who tells us to be good, but never actually leaves coal in our stockings. In fact, he's not even the one who leaves us good things.

✓ God as a celestial cop. Wielding a gun and a stick, his purpose is to catch us making a mistake and then pounce on us with punishment and a lecture.

✓ God as a deal maker. All about contracts, he will do what we want when we do what he wants. Fulfill our obligations to Him and he is obligated to fulfill his to us. Tit for tat.

✓ God as a non-judgmental buddy. He is a friend (read enabler) who just wants us to feel good about life. Never one to make us feel bad, he is always there to listen to us, console us, pat us on the back and tell us we are right. And far be it from him to confront or correct.

✓ God as a joy crusher. Quite opposite of buddy god, this version is an always serious, uptight teacher who sees it as his responsibility to crush all enjoyment. To have a relationship with this version means he will take away everything that we like to do.

✓ God as a puppeteer. Pulling all the strings of the universe, He does things that make no sense, will not explain and does not really care about us or the consequences of His actions. His concern is what He wants and how he can manipulate strings to get it.

✓ God as a guilt inducing, shaming, blaming parent. This version is *that* parent – the one who knows how to make kids feel bad (shame), who makes them feel like problems are always their fault (blame), and who causes them to live with a nagging guilt complex.

Any of those sound a gong? You may have a different description.

I had a wrong view. Even worse, I didn't know I had a wrong view. If confronted, I would have denied it. In fact, I gave a closer to correct description of God while holding a wrong view.

Ripples of the Wrong View of God

My wrong view of God was that of a distant, fault finding, harsh celestial cop combined with demanding, never satisfied, guilt inducing parent. But it was even worse than that. I didn't know I had that wrong view, would have denied it and even taught the right view while holding on to the wrong view. Alarming! One of the most dangerous issues with the wrong pictures of God is that we believe them to be true and normal. We've held them so long we don't even notice them. Like a nagging pain that preoccupied us at first but that we've come to live with, we don't recognize there is a problem.

That subconscious wrong view deep in my soul was slowly killing me as it set my trajectory *away* from God. And I was blind to it. What a mess.

Then came the day of God's plea, "Come, sit on my lap." My response was deep internal pain and fear when I should have been thrilled. It pulled the wrong view from its hiding place into the open. It was disorienting and scary. When your soul cracks, that will happen. Every time I prayed over those six months, God forced me to look at my wrong view of Him. Brought into His light, the false, subconscious paradigm began to fall apart and the real God was revealed. Slowly, the truth of God as loving Heavenly Dad remolded my mind, heart and soul. Lies cannot endure God's truth. Darkness cannot endure light.

The false view of God was the barrier that caused me to refuse God's plea, "Come, sit on my lap." Once the subconscious paradigm was brought into the open, the truth of who God actually is overwhelmed the lies. Sitting on God's lap began to change everything.

Real Life Begins

I began to experience life, real life.

> And this is eternal life, that they know you, the only true God, and Jesus Christ whom you have sent. -- John 17:3

In John 17:3, Jesus describes that real life as "eternal life." He is referring to our souls being brought back to life *now*, not in Heaven. Eternal life begins when we accept the invitation to relationship with God through Jesus and goes on into Heaven.

Jesus not only describes that life, but also defines it: "that they ***know*** you." Real life, eternal life, is knowing God and Jesus Christ. The word, "know" is a word of intimacy. It is the same root word used in the Christmas story when Joseph refrained from physical intimacy with Mary (i.e., "knew her not") until after Jesus' birth.

> When Joseph woke from sleep, he did as the angel of the Lord commanded him: he took his wife, but knew her not until she had given birth to a son. -- Matthew 1:24-25a

Every wrong view of God prevents us from experiencing the true, deep relationship God created. As we recognize those wrong views, we open the possibility of adopting the right view of God.

CHAPTER SEVEN

THE RIGHT PICTURE OF GOD

To sit on God's lap requires that we find and hold on to the right pictures of God

Remember, A.W. Tozer's words, *"What comes to our minds when we think about God is the most important thing about us."*

Having the right view of God is *the* most important thing about us. How we feel, think, act…*everything* is determined by it. There are many attributes of God that can be placed into two categories:

FIRST: God is holy; our role is obedient servants

It all starts here with God as holy and our role as obedient servants.

It is important to understand that the picture of God when He invited me onto His lap was divine, Almighty God seated on His throne. The power of the experience was in the One who called to me. He is first and foremost the God of all that is.

When God appears to people, or when Jesus appears in His glorified form, the first response is fear of His magnificence and, often, belief they are about to die.

> Exalt the Lord our God, and worship at his holy mountain; for the Lord our God is holy!   -- Psalm 99:9

The response to God as holy is to exalt Him, that is, to promote His qualities, to honor as our Lord. It is also to express His worth or value through reverence, adoration, respect and honor, which is the true meaning of worship.

> Thus says the Lord: "Heaven is my throne, and the earth is my footstool;   -- Isaiah 66:1a

To see God as holy is to view Him as Almighty God seated on the throne of Heaven as if His feet are propped up on the earth.

To see God as holy is to recognize that His enormity is beyond comprehension. We can get but a tiny glimpse of His power, His rule over all that is, His ultimate control. We must remember that we are beings spoke into existence by His voice.

> You call me Teacher and Lord, and you are right, for so I am.
> -- John 13:13

To see God as holy is also to acknowledge Jesus as Savior, Lord, highly exalted, and above all that is.

> Ah, Lord God! It is you who have made the heavens and the earth by your great power and by your outstretched arm! Nothing is too hard for you.   -- Jeremiah 32:17

To see God as holy is to accept God as all-powerful – that there is nothing God cannot do. That which we think impossible is nothing to God.

> Then King David went in and sat before the Lord and said, "Who am I, O Lord God, and what is my house, that you have brought me thus far?   -- 2 Samuel 7:18

When we see God as holy and all powerful, it gives us perspective – that we are nothing compared to Him. We are dust that God put together to make us. With one word, God can create or destroy. Yet we are something because He places value on us.

> for it is written, 'As I live, says the Lord, every knee shall bow to me, and every tongue shall confess to God.' So then each of us will give an account of himself to God.
> -- Romans 14:11–12

Because Almighty God is holy, one day every person *will* bow and honor Him as God. Some do so now, but *all* will eventually.

We must see God as holy, Almighty God before we can relate to Him as loving Heavenly Dad. What value is there to sit on God's lap if He is a powerless imposter?

Awesomeness has to be in God's job description

I know they are well-meaning, that the pressure is on and they are not trained to help in crisis and grief. I appreciate their effort. But…sometimes people are not helpful when I'm going through hard stuff.

"It's going to be okay…it will all work out," they say, but it doesn't. And how can it be "okay" when a loved one died tragically and is not coming through the front door again? When the diagnosis is terminal? When the abuse cannot be undone? The words are empty because those people, as much as they love and are trying to reassure, are *powerless* to change the circumstances. If I were ruder I would shout, "No it is not and why are you lying to me?"

If God is not holy, Almighty God, then He is just like those people. If His arms are not all-powerful to love and protect, it does no good to sit on His lap.

Ah, **but He IS holy, Almighty God!** Awe of God then allows us to move to intimacy.

> The Lord your God is in your midst, a mighty one who will save; he will rejoice over you with gladness; he will quiet you by his love; he will exult over you with loud singing.
> -- Zephaniah 3:17

SECOND: God is Heavenly Dad; our identity is children

"We don't see things as they are; we see them as we are."

That centuries old Jewish proverb is especially important for this topic of our identity and relationship with God.

A child will respond to his dad with whom he has experienced a loving relationship with delight. The same child will have the opposite reaction to a stranger even if that man is a more loving dad to his children than his own father. The child's response is determined by the child's identity with and relationship to each adult, not the character of the man.

For those whose picture of God is a stranger, distant relative, cosmic cop, or puppeteer, they will respond very differently than those whose picture of God is a loving Heavenly Dad. *That* is why it is absolutely essential that we see God as He really is. EVERYTHING hangs on it.

> Anyone who does not love does not know God, because God is love.
> -- 1 John 4:8

The above scripture identifies God's nature as love. The Bible provides many characteristics of God that point to God as holy, but it has only one descriptor of His nature: love.

> For you did not receive the spirit of slavery to fall back into fear, but you have received the Spirit of adoption as sons, by whom we cry, 'Abba! Father!' The Spirit himself bears witness with our spirit that we are children of God, and if children, then heirs—heirs of God and fellow heirs with Christ, provided we suffer with him in order that we may also be glorified with him.
> -- Romans 8:15–17

Romans 8 shows us that our identity with God is as children who are everything to their Dad. Verse 15 specifically states that our relationship with God is not to be one of fear, but as a dearly cherished child. "Abba" is a term of intimate familiarity, similar to "Papa" or "Daddy." It is the word Jesus used when in deep pain in the Garden of Gethsemane when He was facing a cruel death.

Our role with holy God is as obedient servant. Our identity and relationship with loving Heavenly Dad is cherished children.

To experience God as holy is to be in reverent awe. To experience God as loving Heavenly Dad is to be relationally intimate.

To approach God as holy is to bow at His feet. To approach God as loving Heavenly Dad is to sit on His lap.

Without the all-powerful strength God has as holy, sitting on His lap does not work. Without the indescribable love God has as Heavenly Dad, bowing at His feet doesn't work.

Jesus chooses a mascot

Jesus chose a nickname for His followers. After walking in human form for over 30 years and after leading His movement for a while, He chose a term that would be the designation, a kind of mascot for His group. Deliberately. Intentionally. Carefully. Purposefully. A name to define their identity. One would expect Him to choose a word similar to the strong words He used in His mission statement. Proclaim good news, declare liberty to captives, give sight to the blind and set free the oppressed.

> The Spirit of the Lord is upon me, because he has anointed me to proclaim good news to the poor. He has sent me to proclaim liberty to the captives and recovering of sight to the blind, to set at liberty those who are oppressed, -- Luke 4:18

That kind of powerful language calls for a mascot full of power and victory. Mighty Warriors. Roaring Lions. Soaring Eagles. Fighting Bulldogs. And yet, what we read in red letters is, well, surprising, unflattering, even disheartening. Where most mascots capture how team members are to perform, Jesus chooses a phrase to describe who we are to God and Who He is to us.

"Little children." Yeah, I know. A shock for the disciples, I'll bet. And none too flattering.

"Little children?" Really?

Yes. And it describes us well. It wasn't a suggestion, a slip of the tongue, or an option. If a person was to follow Jesus, becoming a little child was *the* requirement because to belong to Jesus started and ended with being in relationship with God as Father to a *little* child.

Until I was willing to crawl onto God's lap as a little child, it was impossible for me to experience the "kingdom" life of relationship with God.

> Truly, I say to you, unless you turn and become like children, you will never enter the kingdom of heaven.
> -- Matthew 18:3

Understand, it is an endearing term that didn't spontaneously slip out of Jesus' mouth. It is the intentional phrase that Jesus, who is God, used to define our identity and our relationship with God. "Little children" calculatedly names who God wants to be to us and who we must be to Him, if we choose to be in relationship.

By defining us as "little children," Jesus simultaneously defines God as *Loving Heavenly Dad.* That true view of God *must* be the lens through which we see Him. And it changes everything.

Who enjoys it more?

Let's go deeper. What does a little child do with a loving father? Where does she seat herself? Where do they want to be with daddy when scared or hurt or tired? In daddy's lap. It's what little children do. It's what little children are *created* to do. And it is what you and I are created to do with our loving, Heavenly Dad. His lap is where we belong.

As I write, our oldest grandchild, Brodie, is seventeen months old. He is often at our house when I arrive home from work. As soon as he spots me at the door, exhilaration takes over his body. He smiles and *runs* to me. Barely in the house and before I can set my briefcase down, he is in front of me, ready for Grandpa's arms. And he can't stand still. The excitement, the anticipation, the coming joy of being in Grandpa's arms is too much. So he moves, his little legs running, running, running in place until he and Grandpa happily hug.

Guess who is thrilled most? Grandpa. As much as Brodie loves being held, I love it more. As much as delight dances in Brodie's eyes, the delight in my eyes is brighter. As Brodie runs in place with anticipation, my heart runs harder. As much pleasure Brodie gets from being held, my pleasure is greater.

And so it is with God.

Parents and grandparents find it easy to identify with my delight holding Brodie. So why do we find it difficult to believe we bring the same to God? He created human beings to share a love relationship that would bring deep satisfaction to both Himself and people. The original design has not changed.

As much as we long for God's lap, God longs more. As much satisfaction as we get from being with God, He gets more. We delight our loving Heavenly Dad when we run in place crying out, "Daddy!"

Holy God, loving Heavenly Dad. Those combined make up the right view of God.

Both/And

Crawling onto God's lap is saying "Yes" to closeness with God as loving Heavenly Dad. It is tender, loving, accepting, healing, transforming, renewing, and brings your soul back to life. Crawling onto

God's lap is also saying "Yes" as obedient servants to holy, Almighty God who extends the invitation. The *real* God: holy, all-powerful, all-knowing, all-present, eternal, sovereign, just, rescuing and protecting through the sacrifice of Jesus. He is King of kings and Lord of lords, to be honored and obeyed. It is not either/or. It is both/and.

And, is better than we can imagine!

CHAPTER EIGHT

LETTING JESUS BE GOD-SIZED

To sit on God's lap means we allow Jesus to expand His Presence to occupy more and more of our hearts and lives

A girl of ten years went with a group of family and friends to see the Christmas light displays at various locations throughout the city. At one church building, they stopped and got out to look more closely at a beautifully done nativity scene.

"Isn't that beautiful?" said the little girl's grandmother. "Look at all the animals, Mary, Joseph and the baby Jesus."

"Yes, Grandma," replied the granddaughter. "It is really nice. But there is only one thing that bothers me. Isn't baby Jesus ever going to grow up? He's the *same size* he was last year."

Is Jesus the same size for you as He was last year? Does He occupy the same space as He did 365 days ago? In your heart? Your mind? Your soul? Or is He smaller, with less control of your life?

This is not about Christmas, although that particular season can be one of the hardest in which to keep Jesus at the center. This is about all the seasons of the year and every season of life.

As you read this chapter, reflect on the past month and year. Are you intentionally *making* the effort to allow Jesus to get bigger in your life or are the circumstances in life causing Him to have a smaller part of your life? Are you being pulled toward Him or allowing Him to be pushed away?

Sadly, for many, Jesus doesn't stand a chance. There are good moments with Jesus, but the overall experience of life pushes Him away. Doesn't have to be that way, it's a choice. When we allow Jesus to get bigger, it is incredibly better for us.

How do we do it? It's not complicated, but takes effort. Mary knew the way:

> But the angel said to her, 'Do not be afraid, Mary, you have found favor with God. You will be with child and give birth to a son, and you are to give him the name Jesus. He will be great and will be

called the Son of the Most High. The Lord God will give him the throne of his father David, and he will reign over the house of Jacob forever; his kingdom will never end.'

'How will this be,' Mary asked the angel, 'since I am a virgin?'

The angel answered, 'The Holy Spirit will come upon you, and the power of the Most High will overshadow you. So the holy one to be born will be called the Son of God. Even Elizabeth your relative is going to have a child in her old age, and she who was said to be barren is in her sixth month. For nothing is impossible with God.'

'I am the Lord's servant,' Mary answered. 'May it be to me as you have said.' Then the angel left her.
-- Luke 1:30–38

Notice that the action Mary took that opened up her life to be miraculous was simply to say "Yes." She didn't have great feats to accomplish or acts of worship to perform. God was asking for a simple "Yes," with the offer that He would do the rest.

Ways to say "Yes!"

This is also true for us. Saying "Yes" to God in the following ways all year long will cause Jesus to grow bigger.

1. Time with God.

What better gift can we give to people than our time? What better gift can we give to Jesus than to spend time with Him? Ironically, by taking time to be with God, we receive His peace, contentment, strength, guidance and so much more. Saying "Yes" to time with God is about relationship, just *being together*. This includes: time in conversation, listening and speaking; time reading the Bible, listening to Him and learning about Him; time in worship; and time in service to others. It's all about time – getting to know and love Him in personal relationship. That will make Him bigger.

2. Living life God's way.
Say "Yes" to intentionally living life with a God focus. It means going against the self-focused, consumer driven culture to live with an other-focused, Holy Spirit driven lifestyle. It requires that every day we surrender the throne of our lives and invite Jesus to sit and rule there. Then we live it, in all we do, in every way throughout the day. Ironically, we discover true satisfaction when we do. By so living, we give Jesus His proper place and He will get bigger.

3. Seize salt, light and fragrance opportunities.
God is always working. We must pay attention and then join God in pointing people to Jesus by bringing flavor, understanding and the sweet scent of Jesus everywhere we go and in all we do. As we spend time with Him and focus on Him, Jesus will be at the forefront of our minds. Acting like and talking about Jesus is the natural result. *That* is the heart of God and will do more to make Him bigger than anything else we can do.

Think about one year from today's date. Do you want to hit that day weary, exhausted, empty and with a smaller Jesus in your soul? Or would you like to be better, stronger, spiritually fresher, mentally renewed, emotionally filled and with a bigger Jesus to propel you forward?

Mary said "Yes." Her life, Joseph's life, and the world were never the same. The "yes" was followed by great joy, hard times, deep sorrow, and challenging sacrifices. And amazement that continues into Heaven.

The same can happen for you. Your choice.

Part Two: The True View of God

CHAPTER NINE

PIGS IN A BLANKET

To sit on God's lap allows God to show us what is really real

Centuries ago, Sheila and I were preparing for our wedding.

"How about if we have pigs in a blanket at the wedding?" she asked.

I thought it rather strange that sausages wrapped in a pancake would be served at a wedding reception. But it was Toledo…in a Polish family…and not the first time I discovered something odd about my wonderful fiancée…and she was the bride, so I agreed.

Months later, we were walking hand in hand out of the sanctuary where, for some reason beyond my understanding, Sheila had said "I do" when asked if she took me to be her husband.

"You need to get into the fellowship hall, **now!** They're ready to serve the food," my brand new mother-in-law exclaimed.

First in line (being the bride and groom has its privileges), we gathered our food at the buffet. I saw all the food we had requested except the pigs in a blanket. In their place were rolls of cabbage stuffed with hamburger covered in a red sauce.

"Where are the pigs in a blanket?" I whispered to the woman in white.

"Right there!"

"Right where?" Perhaps love really had blinded me. "I don't see them."

Sheila poked her fork at the cabbage rolls, "Right *there*!"

"Those aren't pigs in a blanket," I responded. "Pigs in a blanket are sausages wrapped in pancakes."

"Why would we have sausages and pancakes at our wedding reception?"

"That's what I wondered when you asked to have them months ago. But, hey, it's your wedding."

"That's just silly. Eat your pigs in a blanket and be happy."

The ink hadn't dried on the marriage license and already we had our first argument.

Who won the argument? Don't go there.

Who was right? Both of us. In southern Ohio, pigs in a blanket are sausages wrapped in pancakes. In northern Ohio, they are hamburger wrapped in cabbage.

Neither of us thought to describe pigs in a blanket because we *knew* what they are and never thought they were anything except what we knew. We were both blind to the reality of the other person.

Is it possible we have grown up in a world so upside down from God's reality that we are blind to what is true? It's not that we ever intended to be, it's just that we have not spent enough time with God to see and hear Him describe what is real, what is true, what is valuable, what is important, what we should live for, what will matter while we're alive and when we die. Is it possible that we think we know what God is talking about but will only find out on our "wedding day" (Revelation 21) that we were *way* wrong?

It's not a big deal to know what pigs in a blanket are. It is eternally essential to know what God says is really real.

> What is highly valued among men is detestable in God's sight.
> -- Luke 16:15b (NIV)

> for we walk by faith, not by sight.   -- 2 Corinthians 5:7

PART THREE

When Jesus Shows Up

CHAPTER TEN

AMAZING THINGS HAPPEN WHEN JESUS SHOWS UP

To sit on God's lap allows us to see Jesus as He really is

"I wish I could talk with Jesus face to face," I've heard people say. "Then I could really know Him and what He wants." I agree that it is tempting, even natural, to wish Jesus would show up like that. However, I'm not sure it would go quite like we imagine if Jesus showed up as He really is.

For instance, when Peter, James and John experienced Jesus as He really is on the Mount of Transfiguration.

> And after six days Jesus took with him Peter and James, and John his brother, and led them up a high mountain by themselves. And he was transfigured before them, and his face shone like the sun, and his clothes became white as light. And behold, there appeared to them Moses and Elijah, talking with him. And Peter said to Jesus, "Lord, it is good that we are here. If you wish, I will make three tents here, one for you and one for Moses and one for Elijah." He was still speaking when, behold, a bright cloud overshadowed them, and a voice from the cloud said, "This is my beloved Son, with whom I am well pleased; listen to him." When the disciples heard this, they fell on their faces and were terrified. -- Matthew 17:1–6

These were the three guys who knew Jesus best. The guys Jesus chose to accompany Him on this important occasion. And yet, when they saw Him as He really is, they ended up on their faces terrified.

Or the day Jesus emerged alive from the tomb, when He showed up to dozens of people, including those He chose to be His apostles.

> As they were talking about these things, Jesus himself stood among them, and said to them, 'Peace to you!' But they were startled and frightened and thought they saw a spirit.
> -- Luke 24:36–37

If any should have expected it, it would have been these guys. But when He showed up as He really is, they were shaking in their robes and shaking their heads to clear away the hallucination.

Then there's the time Jesus showed up to give the Apostle John the Revelation.

> When I saw him, I fell at his feet as though dead. But he laid his right hand on me, saying, 'Fear not, I am the first and the last,'
> -- Revelation 1:17

John was known as the one Jesus loved. In other words, His best and closest friend. As Jesus died, John was the one man to whom He entrusted the well-being of His mother. And yet, when John saw Jesus as He really is, he fainted dead away.

The real Jesus still shows up, usually not quite so dramatically, but in similarly powerful ways. He *wants* to show up in our lives for our good and His glory. When He does, there is a consistent pattern.

We can describe what happens when the real Jesus shows up in four words. Well, four exclamations that technically have five words:

WHAT?!   *WHOA!*   *WOW!*   *WILL DO.*

It happened when Jesus took Peter, James and John up the mountain and was transfigured into His glorified self.

It happened when the disciples saw Jesus after He rose from dead to alive.

It happened to the Apostle John in Revelation 1.

Responding this way leads to the incredible. It doesn't start that way, but when people stay with it, there is always more than they bargained for.

Let me expound. When the real Jesus in His glorified form reveals himself to people, there is a clear sequence to their responses. It goes something like this.

Baffled, they exclaim, "WHAT?!"

First they are baffled at the sight of Jesus. That is, befuddled, confused, dazed, bewildered, disoriented. It will cause our eyes to cross, our tongues to freeze and our brains to question what is real. Disoriented is a good description because when you come face to face with God, things don't make sense. This is hard because we tend to think that if Jesus would ever show up, everything would then make sense. Usually the opposite is true.

If there was a picture with a caption or a soundtrack to the moment, it would sound something like, **"WHAT?!"**

Awed, they exclaim, "WHOA!"

Next, they are in awe when they begin to grasp what is happening. They experience a combination of wonder, amazement, and reverence. Often speechless, they are always inadequate to fully comprehend or sufficiently describe. It is a taste of His holiness, His power and His transcendence. Most often people think, "This just can't be. It's impossible," followed by finding themselves face down on the ground, overwhelmed. Some even believe they will die in holy fear.

The soundtrack, **"WHOA!"**

Gaining Confidence, they exclaim, "WOW!"

After that, they gain confidence as Jesus works and speaks, experiencing trust, assurance, belief, certainty, conviction. Not confidence in themselves, their circumstances, or even understanding of the situation but rather confidence that Jesus is God and is in control. With remnants of awe and bafflement, they gain profound confidence that God is God, that He is all-powerful and, most importantly, that He is on their side. The experience transforms people. When people see Jesus' magnitude, all else shrinks.

The soundtrack, **"WOW!"**

Receiving Instructions, they exclaim, "WILL DO."

Finally, they receive instructions to participate in Jesus' plan: His directions, marching orders, commands, next steps. After moving through the experiences of bafflement, awe and confidence in Jesus, it is finally possible to clearly hear His instructions. They then have the choice to obey or refuse. Some turn away, but most who make it to this moment obey boldly, convinced that God is Almighty, all-loving and knows what is best. It makes no sense to *cross* all powerful God nor *disappoint* all loving God.

The soundtrack, **"WILL DO."**

The purpose of *bafflement* is to clear us of old ways of thinking that get in the way by disorienting us and reorienting us to Jesus.

The purpose of *awe* is to remove any doubt that Jesus really is all-powerful God, causing us to be open to whatever He is up to.

The purpose of gaining *confidence* in Jesus Christ is to shift our trust from ourselves to Christ, relying on Him completely, knowing that He is in control and will handle whatever comes.

The purpose of receiving *instructions* is to clearly know what we are to do to to follow Christ, boldly joining Him in the incredible life and work He offers.

When Jesus shows up, it not just to show off. Rather, it is so we can know Him better and join Him in His work. It was part of the transformation of the first disciples. It can be for us as well.

Part Three: When Jesus Shows Up

CHAPTER ELEVEN

WHEN GOD IS WORKING MOST

To sit on God's lap causes us to lean into Him when life unravels and we want to take control

As I prayed, I heard the words. While walking through dark days and watching people I care about live through unraveling times, I heard the message that was clearly from God:

> ***When things appear to be unraveling the worst,***
> ***God is often working the most.***

Dark days and unraveling times are when we're tempted to think God has turned His head, or stepped out for coffee, or is taking a nap. You've been there. Maybe you're there now.

Yet…dark days and unraveling times are when God is often working the most. It's counter intuitive. Feels upside down, but it is true.

The problem is that we can't see what is going on beyond earth. We can only observe the physically observable, hear the physically hearable and touch the physically touchable. The unseen is, well, so unseeable. And that is frustrating no matter how much God is working.

The unraveling times are when God invites us to trust Him most. Trust Him that things won't unravel completely, that we won't be left with the end of the yarn of our lives jerked out of our hands and destroyed. Getting us to ***trust*** that He is "working the most" is exactly why God won't let us know all that He is doing during those unraveling days. If we know how God is going to work things out, trust is removed from the equation. When you already know the final score, you are much less invested when you watch a recording of a game. Trust is the primary quality God wants to build into us.

How could Abraham trust that God would deliver Isaac from the fiery altar? It sure looked like Abraham's plans and dreams were unraveling. But He saw God do "a working the most" miracle. How? By trusting Him.

How could Joseph experience the fulfillment of the God-promised dreams God had tucked into Joseph's heart? It sure looked like Joseph's life was unraveling as he was sold into slavery, wrongfully accused of accosting his master's wife, forgotten by a friend, and separated from his family for decades. But he watched God do a "working the most" miracle as he became vice-Pharaoh of the world. How? By trusting Him.

How could Peter walk through doors and past soldiers like a ghost? It sure looked like he had the last inch of life's yarn in his hand when he was arrested and awaiting death. His friend and fellow apostle had already been killed and Peter's name was next on Herod's hatchet list. But God was up to one of those "working the most" moments and miraculously saved him from certain death. How? By Peter trusting Him.

The biggest unraveling of all was when Jesus headed to the cross. The whole world thought it was over, that Jesus had forfeit the opportunity to be their king, as they watched Him die on the cross. Not only did it appear that everything had unraveled for Jesus, it looked like it had come apart for everyone else. But God was "working the most" when He resurrected Jesus on Easter. How could it happen? Because Jesus trusted the Father.

> ***When things appear to be unraveling the worst, God is often working the most.***

Now take another look at those things that are unraveling in your life. Anything come close to being asked to sacrificially kill your child, being wrongfully imprisoned for nearly two decades in the prime of your life, being placed on death row by a lunatic dictator, or dying on a cross as your Father watches? I don't think so. It might *feel* like it, but my guess is it doesn't come close. Even if it does, God is *still* working.

So as you watch things appear to unravel in the worst ways, will you trust God to work the most? Trust Him as Abraham, Joseph, Peter and Jesus did–by obeying what He says completely. Trust by allowing Him to work out the future His way. And, as my mom would say, "Keep your cotton picking hands off of it!" Trust Him by holding your tongue when you want to give God advice. Just put the threads that have unraveled and the cloth that is still intact in His hands by praying, worshipping, listening to His Word, serving others, being faithful and putting one foot in front of the other with confident trust.

Part Three: When Jesus Shows Up

Oh, and don't forget to keep your eyes open. Because you *will* see God come through. *Always*. And better than you can imagine.

As you trust Him.

And we know that for those who love God all things work together for good, for those who are called according to his purpose.
-- Romans 8:28

For I know the plans I have for you, declares the Lord, plans for welfare and not for evil, to give you a future and a hope.
-- Jeremiah 29:11

CHAPTER TWELVE

THE VERY, VERY, WORST & BEST DAY OF ALL

To sit on God's lap leads us to look forward to the day when we will see Him face to face

I've had some bad days. You've had some bad days. Everyone has had bad days.

When my oldest child was a toddler, we thought it would be nice to get his picture sitting on the Easter Bunny's lap at the local department store. He took one look at the 7-foot creature, hairy arms and long ears and wanted no part of whatever it was. We coaxed, bribed, and begged to no avail. Being cruel parents, we put him on the monster's lap for a moment anyway. Just to snap one quick picture. How else would we remember this all important first Easter? It is not a hallmark photo. That was a very bad day for the child. Scarred him for life.

As adults, we look at that bad day for Andrew and probably think, "Get a grip. That was not a bad day. Not even close."

Another child came home crying. A couple of friends had called her a name. She was rejected and dejected. The hurt was deep, inflicted by girls who were supposed to be her friends. I asked her what name they had called her. She told me. I asked her to repeat it. She did. I asked her several more times. Each time she enunciated the same syllables. I had trouble keeping a straight face. It wasn't a name at all. Unless it was in another language… from another planet... in another universe. They'd made it up. But it was a very bad day for the child.

As adults, we look at that bad day for Carissa and probably think, "Get a grip. That was not a bad day. Not even close."

Where is the Hope?

Folks all around us are having much worse days – losing loved ones, losing jobs, losing health, losing independence. Some are struggling to just survive. As I listen to peoples' problems, hear their hurt, and watch their tears, I understand that there are a lot of bad days. Some much worse than others, but all painful. Tragedies often force us to realize that what we thought was bad was actually pretty good, or at least not as bad as we thought.

Where is the hope? Do we all just throw in the towel? Do we live in fear that the next day may be worse? Is there some perspective to help us live more boldly?

Bad is a relative word. The word only makes sense in the context of comparison. You're having a bad day? Compared to what? Compared to a child being seated on a big rabbit's lap? Compared to a child called a mythical name? Compared to a family who lost their dad, husband, son, primary income, and stability?

Here is the hope: There is a day in the future that will make the very worst day we ever have pale in comparison. That day will make our nastiest experience seem like a big gentle rabbit. We don't know when it will arrive, but it will knock on every door. I'm talking about THE day. Here it is...

> Just as man is destined to die once, and after that to face judgment,
> -- Hebrews 9:27

THAT Day

Yep, I'm talking about *that* day when each of us will breathe our last and leave the physical body we've moved around in. We will come face to face with God and be evaluated. That day will make our worst day fade away regardless of which of the two directions it takes you.

If you are living in relationship with God through Jesus Christ, having turned your back on sin and striving to be obedient, you will experience an ecstasy the Bible can't begin to describe. All those bad days will be gone forever and you will enjoy a life of eternal ecstasy. It will be the *very, very BEST day of all.*

But if you are living for yourself, absent from a relationship with God but insisting on your own way (sin), you will experience a pain the Bible can't begin to describe. All the bad days, no matter how deep the pain, will seem as nothing compared to the agony described as eternal burning. Burning that never pauses. That is never soothed. That never ends. It will be the *very, very WORST day of all.*

So, what are you going to do with that? The day is coming. You might avoid taxes, but death is going to get you. God wants that day to be the *best* day for you. He did not create you for hell, He created you for heaven. He wants you to accept His forgiveness and allow Jesus to pay for your sins by living in relationship with Him.

Don't assume you are okay because you are a good person or go to church or pray or read the Bible. It is all about *relationship* with God through Jesus, not about doing things. Accept that relationship by turning to God and away from sin. God wants your friendship for all eternity and He's covered the costs. Ask for forgiveness, and begin to live in relationship with Him. Then there will be no reason to fear and every reason to live with joy.

> But if we walk in the light, as he is in the light, we have fellowship with one another, and the blood of Jesus, his Son, purifies us from all sin. If we claim to be without sin, we deceive ourselves and the truth is not in us. If we confess our sins, he is faithful and just and will forgive us our sins and purify us from all unrighteousness.   -- 1 John 1:7-9

Part Three: When Jesus Shows Up

CHAPTER THIRTEEN
JESUS WAS ALWAYS PICKING FIGHTS

To sit on God's lap means we join Jesus in confronting wrong

Here's a topic you won't hear a lot of people mention when they refer to Jesus. But it is true! Jesus was always picking fights. Search the accounts of His life and you will find it was His lifestyle. It wasn't that conflicts blindsided Him or that He couldn't avoid them. It was that Jesus *initiated* skirmishes. A lot. Along with the teaching, miracles, healings, and other eye-popping moments, time after time He intentionally picked fights with the authorities. He seemed to be itching for a fight. I know – when we consider how Jesus has been portrayed most of our lives, it stretches us to see Him as constantly "taking it outside."

Jesus even did so in His hometown. The first time back after His baptism, desert temptation and beginning of His ministry, He right away created a brawl. Seems to me it would be the time to let people know that the kid they watched grow up had actually been the Son of God incognito by doing something nice. But, NO! He picks a fight.

> And getting into a boat he crossed over and came to his own city. And behold, some people brought to him a paralytic, lying on a bed. And when Jesus saw their faith, he said to the paralytic, 'Take heart, my son; your sins are forgiven.' And behold, some of the scribes said to themselves, 'This man is blaspheming.' But Jesus, knowing their thoughts, said, 'Why do you think evil in your hearts? For which is easier, to say, "Your sins are forgiven," or to say, "Rise and walk"? But that you may know that the Son of Man has authority on earth to forgive sins'—he then said to the paralytic—'Rise, pick up your bed and go home.' And he rose and went home. When the crowds saw it, they were afraid, and they glorified God, who had given such authority to men.
> -- Matthew 9:1–8

At first glance, it appears He was picking fights with people He grew up with, but it was not the people. He was acting in love toward the people by picking fights with wrong beliefs that led to wrong actions. Picking fights with falsehoods was part of His mandate to help people discover the *real* God! That is not the typical image of Jesus.

On another occasion, Jesus intentionally defied the religious rules of the day that which had led to a wrong view of God and His ways.

> Again he entered the synagogue, and a man was there with a withered hand. And they watched Jesus, to see whether he would heal him on the Sabbath, so that they might accuse him. And he said to the man with the withered hand, 'Come here.' And he said to them, 'Is it lawful on the Sabbath to do good or to do harm, to save life or to kill?' But they were silent. And he looked around at them with anger, grieved at their hardness of heart, and said to the man, 'Stretch out your hand.' He stretched it out, and his hand was restored. The Pharisees went out and immediately held counsel with the Herodians against him, how to destroy him.
> -- Mark 3:1–6

Did you see it? Jesus picked a fight, angry at the religious leaders for falsely applying God's law. As a result, their actions had caused people unnecessary burdens and would have left the man with a withered hand for life when healing was standing right in front of him. Jesus was drew a line in the sand for God and His purposes. He knew *exactly* what He was doing and where it would lead. Losing the fight, the Pharisees and the Herodians hatched a plot to snuff Jesus out.

If we follow Jesus, we will have to pick fights as well. Being Jesus' disciple means we strap on the armor of God (Ephesians 6:10-18), and go at it as Jesus did. If we fail to reveal falsehood by our words and actions, we are, by omission, allowing lies to stand unchallenged. That is tantamount to mutiny, treason or running in cowardice from the battles Jesus is fighting. Failure to step up to the fight is to fail to live lives of truth by being the salt, light and fragrance of Christ.

It was not really about picking fights for Jesus. It was about putting light on the lies of the enemy that were hurting people. To follow Jesus into such fights is one of the ways we "speak the truth in love" (Ephesians 4:15) for the good of people and the glory of Christ. Even more forcefully, it is part of our mandate.

So…go be like Jesus and pick some fights!

> For we do not wrestle against flesh and blood, but against the rulers, against the authorities, against the cosmic powers over this present darkness, against the spiritual forces of evil in the heavenly places. -- Ephesians 6:12

PART FOUR

Holy and Holding

CHAPTER FOURTEEN

CAN GOD BE BOTH POWER AND LOVE?

To sit on God's lap means we revel in relationship with our loving Heavenly Dad instead of always trying to figure Him out

This is an important issue. Does the idea of being on God's lap reduce God's greatness? His perfection? His position as God of the universe? His role as Master, Savior, Lord at whose feet we should bow? Does intimacy with God contradict the Biblical commands to obey, worship, serve, honor, submit and live for Him?

You may, like me, struggle with the idea that God wants you on His lap. Believe me, I understand.

Power and Love Together

Counter-intuitively, being on God's lap and bowing before Him as holy are not mutually exclusive. One does not eliminate the possibility of the other.

The Sports Illustrated website[4] has a series of pictures of professional athletes with their children. It is a touching portrayal of the tenderness and love these successful adults have for the little people they brought into this world. I love the smiles, hugs, fun, and obvious familiarity the kids have with their famous dads and moms. As it is with all kids, they are not impressed with the high social standing of their parents. The children don't even know there is something special about the ones holding them; it is just dad or mom. Several of the pictures leapt at me.

Manny Pacquiao and daughters Mary and Queen. Here's a man who makes a living by beating other men up. Blackens their eyes. Makes them bleed. Is cheered when his opponent is laid out on the boxing mat, especially if that man is unconscious. (I'm not condoning the sport; just stating facts.) Yet this world class boxer gently invites the hugs of his toddlers. Though magnificently strong, his two little ladies have no fear.

Andy Dalton and son Noah. In a football stadium filled with 80,000 fans, bright lights blazing, Andy stands near smiling fans holding five month-old Noah. The photograph captures the moment when Andy, holding Noah close to his chest, gently kisses the top of his head. Oblivious to the hoopla, Noah scratches and drools on Andy's jersey. This 6'2", 220 pound rough and tough quarterback for the NFL Cincinnati Bengals is famous, rich, successful, and strong. Yet, instead of Noah being in awe or in fear, he feels safe and loved and knows that in his daddy's arms is where he belongs.

Nate Solder and son Hudson. On a practice field, this 6' 9", 325 pound monster of a man lifts his one year-old son, Hudson, into the air. The blonde-haired boy's face is pure delight as he views the world from ten feet in the air, safe in his daddy's grip. In fact, there is matching glee on both faces. Though Nate's arms are the size of Hudson's waist, there is no awe or fear. If Hudson were to fall he could get seriously hurt; but he is oblivious to the danger and full of pleasure because his daddy's power and ability are used for Hudson's good.

None of those children have done anything to earn their daddy's love, nor have they added materially to the family's well being. In fact, as with any child, they have brought disruption and work. And sometimes pain and grief. You see, Hudson has been battling cancer since he was three months old. At the time of the picture, he was receiving chemotherapy treatments every three weeks. I can't even imagine the tears and heartbreak that kick down the door of a parent's heart with that condition. Nate and his wife give even *more* attention, make *more* sacrifices, go to *greater* lengths to care for Hudson because of illness. And hold him on their laps *more* often. Because he belongs there.

Bowing and Being Held Are Not Opposites

There is no contradiction between the power and the love of these three fathers. Each man's strength is obvious as is his love when he is with his child. Both qualities exist in the same person, but it is his love that rules as he uses his strength to love his child. That's why there is no fear. Vastly different photos are those which capture Manny Pacquiao, Andy Dalton and Nate Solder when facing opponents who want to push them out of the way. With children, these strapping men are tender. With adversaries, they are overwhelmingly tough. It all depends on who the men are dealing with – children or opponents.

There is no contradiction between the power and the love of God. God's strength is obvious as is His love for His children. Both qualities exist in the same person, but it is love that rules as He uses His strength to love His children. That's why there need be no fear. It is a vastly different picture when we see God dealing with those who would be their own god, who want to push God out of the way. With children, Almighty God is tender. With those who insist on being in charge, pitting themselves against God, He is overwhelmingly tough. It all depends on who we choose to be – children or opponents.

A lot depends on which we believe is the dominant quality of God. If we view God first as powerful, we will fear Him. But if we view God first as love, then we are free to receive His love that embraces us with His power. Our sin, failures, false ideas, bad experiences, and more make it a struggle to believe God is for us, that He never makes Himself our adversary. We have no point of reference for a God like this, thus we find it hard to be little children and let God be our loving, Heavenly Daddy.

Which brings us back to God's purpose in giving us the picture of little children with their loving dads. He knew we could understand that even if it wasn't our experience with our own fathers. He knows we cannot grasp His love, but that we are moved to tears when we see the likes of Manny Pacquiao, Andy Dalton and Nate Solder tenderly loving their children. God knows that when we see cancer ridden Hudson being cared for by his hulk-like dad who has tears running down his face, we would get it. So He insists we put ourselves in the place of that small child to grasp just a bit of God's love for us. On His lap. In His arms.

We must get past our human way of thinking to adopt God's ways of working.

The Right Kind of Fear

These three men are powerful and to be feared by opponents. They could easily destroy those kids, without breaking a sweat or even breathing hard. As the children grow up, they will realize how powerful and famous their dads are and the proper response will be respect, obedience, and perhaps awe. But the only time they will need to fear their dads is when they have done something that requires discipline. Otherwise, though those athletes are formidable, scary, even violent to others, their children can confidently stake claim to their daddy's arms of love. They *own* their daddy's laps because they belong there. Not because of anything the children have done or even because they are adorable. It is because of their daddy's love. These children know they are loved, valued, protected, and provided for because their daddies do that.

Fear was distorted when Adam bit into rebellion. For those who are His kids, it is wrong to fear that He will harm us. This fear says that He is the celestial cop getting His kicks out of painfully punishing us and that He uses His power against us.

First of all, the right "fear" for God is that we will break His heart more than we will break His rules. As the Heavenly Dad we love, we fear that we will disappoint Him and cause Him pain.

The right "fear" for God is also a healthy awe, reverence, and respect for who He is – holy, high and lifted up, all knowing, all powerful, all present, sovereign and more. We are to bow before Him as Master of the universe, Lord of all, King of kings. Which is why we don't try to sit on His lap without His invitation. That invitation was extended to us when Jesus came to earth in human form, lived a sinless life, and died on the cross to rise again in triumph over sin, fear, and death. By accepting the relationship with God through Jesus, we receive an invitation to sit on the lap of the Almighty God. He is still holy and powerful, but His nature is love. Because His nature is love, God wants us to have intimacy and alignment with Him more than anything. Sitting on God's lap is one way we lean into intimacy and alignment.

One of the ironies is that the more intimacy we experience with God, the more awe we will have for God. The deeper the love we share with God, the higher we will honor Him as holy. The more we experience our loving, Heavenly Dad's incredible, powerful, beyond comprehension, sometimes miraculous work, our high regard for Him will grow. The more we sit on His lap, the more deeply we will be in awe of Him. It may seem that fear of God and love for God cannot coexist, but the reality is that neither can exist without the other.

> for God gave us a spirit not of fear but of power and love and self-control. --2 Timothy 1:7

Part Four: Holy and Holding

CHAPTER FIFTEEN

IS GOD REALLY THERE?

To sit on God's lap means we know God is always listening, even when we don't hear a response

What are you waiting for?
That is really, really, **really** important to you?
That you've lost sleep over?
That you've talked about with lots of people?
That you've prayed, and *really* prayed about?
That doesn't look good as you gaze at the horizon of the future?
That hurts? Maybe hurts so bad you don't know if you'll survive?
That is moving you to anger (or you're already there)?
All because you're waiting and it doesn't seem like God is paying any attention.

When teenagers, a growth appeared on my kids' ears. It morphed from time to time as technology and style changed, but it was rare when the attachments were not part of their heads. Words directed at them could not make it to their eardrums because music was taking up all available ear space. Thus, verbal missives directed toward them were met with heads nodding in time with music I could not hear, and obliviousness to the presence of their loving father. To achieve communication required physical touch to gain attention and hand motions (not sure where I learned them) to indicate they should remove the technology from at least one ear.

Often the originators of the verbal notifications were in a different room, sometimes a different floor, than those intended to receive. Not realizing that music playing through headphones was blocking the communication, I would volley the words again. Louder. With every attempt, my volume increased. Believing I was being intentionally ignored, the words gained emotion. It was not pretty. Finally, in frustration and impatience I would walk to the location of said teen, bang on their door or tap on their arm, do the hand motions and finally say, "Didn't you hear me calling to you?" To which they would look at me as if I had lost my mind, and condescendingly state, "Of course not. I've got my headphones on." Of course. "What did you want?" "Oh," I would mumble. "I don't remember."

Do you ever wonder if God can't hear you over His music? That maybe there is some device covering His divine ears so that your words cannot make it through? That He is oblivious, doesn't notice you, is out of range? The times when you prayed and waited and nothing happened. When you called again with no reply. When you even raised your voice and still nothing. When you were sure what you were asking for was good and right and wonderful and surely what God would want. And it didn't happen. Maybe you're waiting right now, and wondering.

Don't know about you, but waiting did not come in my personality package. Don't like to sit at red lights, in fast food drive through lanes or construction delays. Don't like to wait through commercials. Shoot, I don't like waiting for a few seconds for the web page to load. Even when I'm reminded that only a couple years ago it would take MINUTES for that same page to load. Don't like to wait on the phone when I'm put on hold or in the "waiting room" at the auto body repair shop or the human body repair shop. Didn't like waiting to grow up and don't like waiting as I get old.

But do you know the hardest waiting? When God does not seem to be interested in what is really, very, extremely important to me. I do have some level of understanding (even if impatient) of waiting on human beings, but God IS God, after all. He is not confined by earthly limitations; therefore, we can only conclude that there is no *physical* reason He would ever have to make us wait. In fact, He can see forward in time to know what we will need decades from now and start the wheels in motion so that at just the right moment on April 8 ten years from now it will be waiting for us. Instead of the other way around. Right? So what's the deal with all the waiting for God to answer our prayers and meet our needs?

Sometimes it feels like He is busy, thus we have to wait. Other times it feels like He doesn't care enough to be interrupted (picture God with headphones on listening to His favorite music). Or it feels like we've fallen out of favor and He is not obligated to answer. So we wait.

Ignored. Unimportant. Abandoned. Is that why we have to wait on God. ***ABSOLUTELY NOT***.

Part Four: Holy and Holding

Truth: *everything* that God does for those following Him is born from His unfathomable love. So anytime, every time, we have to wait on God is because He is working for our good. Sometimes making preparations, sometimes arranging circumstances, sometimes working in and through people. Sometimes we are not ready, sometimes other people are not ready, sometimes the world is not ready. Sometimes what we want is not best for us or for others. Sometimes the situation is about us, other times it is about others.

But *always* what God does or does not do and when He does it is rooted in His love. *ALWAYS*

Waiting is a part of God's plan to accomplish good things, and He will never allow pain to last longer than necessary – if we wait on Him, trusting in Him. If we choose to jump in to take care of it our way, it means we are trusting ourselves instead of God, which means the pain will be longer and deeper. Waiting is tougher on the front end, but taking things into our own hands is tougher on the backend. Either way, life is just sometimes tough. But it is our choice when and how tough it will be.

God's ears are never blocked and we are never ignored. Jump ship or jump into His arms. Which will it be?

> He fulfills the desire of those who fear him; he also hears their cry and saves them.   -- Psalm 145:19

CHAPTER SIXTEEN

JAW-DROPPING GRACE

To sit on God's lap is to bask in inconceivable grace

I am blown away by the way Jesus reached into Peter's life when he was at his worst. Jesus *knew* that Peter would betray Him, would deny Him three times. When Jesus needed His close friend most, Peter turned his back on Jesus the worst. Jesus *knew* Peter would fail Him but believed in Peter anyway.

Jesus erased the evidence that could have gotten Peter the death penalty when He replaced the guard's ear.

Jesus prayed for Peter so he would have the strength to return rather than hang himself as Judas did.

Jesus made eye contact with Peter as the rooster crowed signaling the third denial, reminding Peter that Jesus *knew* it would happen and reminding Peter of Jesus' instructions:

> Simon, Simon, behold, Satan demanded to have you, that he might sift you like wheat, but I have prayed for you that your faith may not fail. And when you have turned again, strengthen your brothers. -- Luke 22:31–32

If Jesus had spoken to Peter when He made eye contact, He risked Peter being taken prisoner as well. Mark Batterson states that Jesus' was not scolding or saying "I told you so!" Rather, Jesus' look said, "Peter, look at Me. I forgave you before you even denied Me. I just want you to know that I haven't given up on you. We're still in this thing together!"[5]

Following His resurrection, Jesus specifically restored Peter with unconditional grace (John 21:15-19). And then the Holy Spirit used Peter and others to turn the world upside-down.

How Can It Be True?

There is something within us that resists Jesus' kind of grace – that undeserved, unearned, favored position with God that causes Him to pour out His love, mercy and forgiveness without end. We don't understand it,

Part Four: Holy and Holding

we can't comprehend it, we have a hard time accepting it when offered, so we try to earn it. Oddly, we reject it or try to change it because we believe it must somehow cost us something.

We grow up believing that you get what you earn; that nothing is free in life. "If it sounds too good to be true, it is," we've been told. And everything comes at a cost. If someone offers you a free gift, you'd better check around for the catch because there has to be one. That's true in the human world and works well in school, at work, at the mall and in contracts. Not so good in relationships.

In relationships, conditional love is the norm. If we want someone's love, there are expectations to fulfill. Act right, give back, live up to it, do what that person wants, etc. It's not that our parents intended to put conditions on their love, it's just what we know – what the whole human race understands and lives.

Which is why it is so hard to catch, believe and embrace God's very different kind of grace and love. We have no point of reference for it. We have no experience with it. It's nearly impossible to give or accept something you've never had. We're unprepared.

But when we see it, it takes our breath away. It either turns us into a puddle or makes us run. Peter was a puddle; Judas ran.

Jesus *knew* Peter would deny Him, an act of betrayal by a friend that would pain Jesus deeply. Yet, Jesus reached to Peter with unconditional love and grace without reserve.

Jesus *knows* you have blown it, will blow it, maybe even are still blowing it right now. And He reaches to you with the same unconditional love and grace.

Nothing short of total rejection on Peter's part could prevent him from experiencing the implausible grace of Jesus. Same with you.

All Peter had to do was stay in the vicinity with Jesus. Same with you.

Peter had to do nothing but stand still as unconditional grace washed over him like life-giving water over a man perishing from thirst. Same with you.

When he expected Jesus' rebuke, Peter got His unconditional love, mercy, acceptance, friendship and restoration. Same with you. When we have blown it, it's easy to picture Jesus scolding us with His holy finger in our faces. And to feel like we deserve it. Which we do. It's much harder to picture God inviting us on to His lap when we are still filthy from our sin.

But that is the true picture. Listen to Jesus words and look at His body language as He worked with Peter. There is not even a reference to how badly Peter had blown it. Jesus simply said, "Follow me!" (John 21:19). Same with you.

Unconditional grace. Unqualified, unrestricted, unreserved, without stipulations or criticism. It was for Peter. It is for you.

I can imagine Peter's knees getting weak and eyes filling with tears as this hard-nosed, brawny fisherman was undone by this grace.

Peter's response was to-the-death loyalty, not to try to earn Jesus' acceptance, but because of the love that that filled his heart in response to this amazing grace. Same for you and me.

God's grace really, really, really is free and better than anything we can imagine. It is too good to be true, yet it **IS** true. For YOU!

> And God is able to make all grace abound to you, so that having all sufficiency in all things at all times, you may abound in every good work.   -- 2 Corinthians 9:8

> For by grace you have been saved through faith. And this is not your own doing; it is the gift of God, not a result of works, so that no one may boast.   -- Ephesians 2:8–9

[Margin note: Shouldn't we too?]

[Handwritten note at bottom: What happens when we fail God? We may "preach" to ourselves about how shameful we've acted. We may feel disgusted. Impatient. We wonder if we will ever get "it" right. But, Perfection will never happen in this life. Too much evil influences our behavior in weak moments. We often judge ourselves like we judge others. But to judge isn't our call. If we are true to Christ, he patiently forgives us, loves us back into his arms. And so we should others too. Unconditional love, restorative grace, that's what Jesus would offer.]

Part Four: Holy and Holding

CHAPTER SEVENTEEN

WHAT IS GOD FEELING?

(Author's note: I wrote the article below immediately following the terrorist attack on September 11, 2001. With our world experiencing tragedies and attacks, I thought it appropriate to include it here.)

To sit on God's lap causes us to hear God's heart and see through His eyes, even when it is not what we expect

Along with millions of others, I listened and watched Tuesday's tragic events unfold. Sheila and I headed for Lancaster, PA, traveling on I-70 through Somerset County. After hearing the report of the fourth plane going down within 40 miles of us, it felt like the world was coming to an end. We turned toward home in shock, horror, sadness, anger, frustration, hurt, and disbelief. I hope your first reaction was to pray. Sheila and I did. Along with millions, our family kept praying.

September 11, 2001 is a day that will live in infamy with Pearl Harbor, the JFK assassination, and the Challenger explosion. Only worse because of the nature of the tragedy and the cruelty of the terrorists.

For the first 24 hours I was in shock, overwhelmed by feelings of being violated, by sadness for the victims, by helplessness in our ability to change what happened. On September 13, I asked God, "What is Your perspective on this tragedy, from where You sit? How do you feel?" He answered me. Frankly, He shocked me and I've hesitated to pass it on. But if I ask, I have to be ready to hear.

It is a risk to share what I heard. I don't want to sound cruel or heartless. What has occurred is a tragedy of enormous proportions. There are thousands of people dead, wounded or have loved ones who are dead or suffering. That is awful. So, please understand I'm not trying to make light of it. I am not insensitive to the pain. But I heard God's Spirit clearly speak two messages. (If you don't like them, you can take it up with God. Remember I am only the middle man.) Here they are…

Message #1

Moments after I asked God to give me His perspective, I heard Him say, "You kill 3,500 innocent Americans every day. Why are you so upset and angry about those killed Tuesday?" I was shocked. I was expecting words of comfort, of direction, of help, or even anger. I heard none of that and was immediately convicted. God's right. He's always right. Why are we so upset when foreign terrorists kill thousands when we do it to ourselves everyday through abortion? The life of an unborn child is just as valuable to God as any of the people who perished in these attacks. In fact, the Bible is clear that God is even more protective of the little ones.

Message #2

"There is something worse than dying physically. It is dying without a relationship with Me and going to Hell." All of heaven welcomed many of the people who died Tuesday into an eternity beyond our wildest imaginations. Those people are better off, they're receiving a reward that will last forever and ever and ever. Others, however, are damned to an eternity beyond our nastiest nightmares because they refused a personal relationship with God through Jesus Christ. That is worse than the cruelest death we will hear about.

God's words to me, as surprising as they were, have helped bring me out of the fog of the tragedy and have given me His bigger picture perspective. Yes it is a tragedy. The ripples will last for decades. The worst may be yet to come, but we must gain perspective. Thousands of people around the world suffer daily. Persecuted Christians perish day after day. People die regularly within blocks of us, sometimes even cruelly. Perhaps, if we are honest with God and ourselves, we will admit that our feelings are selfish. The tragedy has threatened our personal sense of security, our personal comforts, and our self-absorbed way of life. It grabs our attention because of the unthinkable way in which we were attacked and the enormity of the loss. We are shaken. This one hit home where we thought we were safe and secure.

I invite you to refocus with me. Ask God to give you His perspective. Live by His promises not what circumstances seem to say. Absorb these words of hope and assurance in the context of eternity.

Part Four: Holy and Holding

> I have told you these things, so that in me you may have peace. In this world you will have trouble. But take heart! I have overcome the world. -- John 16:33

> And we know that in all things God works for the good of those who love him, who have been called according to his purpose. -- Romans 8:28

I also invite you to put your full trust in God. Only in Him do we have true security. All other kinds of security are myths.

> Some trust in chariots and some in horses, but we trust in the name of the LORD our God. -- Psalms 20:7

Let us be God's hands and feet, His Presence in the world. Whatever we can do, we should do. Pray, give blood, make donations, talk with others about God's desires for people to know Him and invite them to place their hope in God.

But let's keep God's perspective and live for Him daily, as well as in times of tragedy.

→ From God's perspective, perhaps this present day is preparation, a winnowing of the grain, a ripening of the church. Chaos is shaking out the serious believers from the chaff. Those who remain unmoved by earth circumstances will heard in a new era of ripe harvest for the coffers of heaven.

CHAPTER EIGHTEEN

CHARLEY AND THE NIS

To sit on God's lap is to get free from all that displeases our loving Heavenly Dad and hinders us from real life

There once was a boy, or so the story is told, who went for a hike in the woods. He came upon a group of youth, about his age, gathered in a circle. "C'mon over," they invited. Tentatively he walked toward them to notice that each one had a small animal-looking thing. It was tiny, furry, and friendly, crawling over the one who was obviously its owner, nuzzling and purring. He stepped into the circle. Introductions were exchanged. He stared at the animals until one boy laughed and said, "You've never seen one of these before, have you? This is a 'nis'. See, on the side of each are the letters, N, I, S. It's a wonderful pet, easy to care for, and it makes you feel incredible. Here, hold one." With that the boy reached into a box, pulled out a black and white nis and handed it to Charley. It was furry and had a long body. As soon as it touched his hand it crawled up Charley's arm, onto his shoulders and lay across his neck. "It likes you," one of the girls in the circle squealed. Indeed, it did, purring and content. Truth was that Charley liked the nis, too. As it lay across his neck, it radiated warmth that started at Charley's neck, ran down his back and legs, and through his arms. Charley felt good, very good. The warmth lulled him into a twilight relaxed state. There was something about this nis, thought Charley as he sat down to join the others in the circle.

When Charley returned home that night he took the nis with him. Every day it would curl up quietly in a corner until Charley came home and every evening he would spend time with it. He didn't have to feed it, it found food for itself and it seemed to draw energy from their time together. As the days went by, the nis grew. Soon it stretched from one arm to the other when it lay on Charley's shoulders. It still sent good shivers through Charley but he could feel the weight growing, not uncomfortable, but certainly noticeable.

One day Charley was so busy that he didn't spend any time with the nis. The next morning he awoke to find the nis crouched two inches from his face, with a purr that sounded much like a wheeze. Strange, thought Charley. He had never heard that sound before. He picked it up, placed it on his shoulders to realize that it wasn't quite as warm as before. Throughout high school, the nis comforted and seemed to help Charley.

The Descent

As the days moved on, the nis continued to grow. Instead of lying in a corner, it would bother Charley in the morning as he prepared for work, it would greet him at the door when he came home, it would follow him throughout the evening constantly crawling onto Charley's shoulders whether he wanted it to or not. As the nis grew heavier, it also grew colder. In fact, it seemed to suck energy and warmth out of Charley instead of putting it into him. The nis became ever more demanding. It was staring Charley in the face when he awoke, when he ate, when he read, whenever he did anything. And it seemed to be losing its soft fur and the once-alluring purr was sounding more and more like a hiss.

Charley didn't know how it accomplished such a feat, but one Tuesday he answered the phone at work to hear a hiss calling his name. He thought it was a prank call and was about to hang up when he recognized the sound. No, it couldn't be, he thought. He listened. It was, but how? This creature was calling him at work. As he listened he felt the weight of his nis upon his shoulders though it was not there and his shoulders sagged. Every day the call would come. Sometimes several times a day. His production decreased, his mood declined, and his relationships suffered.

A couple weeks later, having awakened, washed, shaved, and eaten to the stare and hiss of this animal, he headed for the door looking forward to the privacy of his ride to work. In front of the door stood the nis, blocking Charley's path. Having grown to the size of a Labrador, it was impossible to step over. Charley walked to the back door, but the nis raced to block it. To the side door, the garage door, the same. When Charley tried to push it out of the way, it bit him. Charley was not seriously hurt, but shocked. This was not what he had brought home so many years before. "Just this once I'll stay home from work with you," said Charley, thinking perhaps the nis was sick. All day it lay around his neck, sinking him deeply into the couch.

The next day the nis attempted to block Charley's way. He knew he could not stay home from work so he resignedly placed a leash on it and took it with him to work. Though no one seemed to notice or perhaps care, it was a pain to have the nis at work. It went wherever he did, staring and hissing and weighing him down. Charley's productivity, already declining from the impact of the phone calls, nose dived with the thing actually at work. Yet he couldn't get out the door without it. At the end of the week Charley's boss pulled him aside. "I don't know what's going on, son. You used to be such a good worker, but lately, well… If you don't pick it up, I'm afraid we'll have to let you go." So that was it, the nis was going to get Charley fired.

And as for relationships, that was a bigger problem. Charley's friends had at first thought the nis was cute, but as it grew and began to hiss, they refused to be around it. They feared it and warned Charley it was taking over his house and his life, but he didn't believe them. Some of Charley's other friends had their own nises. They, too, had discovered they couldn't get out of the house without theirs. And his girlfriend had long ago given him an ultimatum. He hadn't intentionally chosen the nis over his girlfriend. It was just simply that as much as he tried, Charley couldn't part with it. So alone he was. With his nis.

Even on Sundays, when he went to church, it was there. Charley would try to leave the nis at home, but it would somehow always go with him. It seemed to especially bother him there. Charley would try to listen to the sermon or lesson or words of encouragement from a friend, but the hiss would get so loud he couldn't concentrate.

The Truth

He was thinking about all this, how his life had not gone as he had imagined and how the nis was the source of so many of these problems when he felt the nis on his shoulders and strangely around his neck. When he reached up to his throat, he realized that instead of draped across his shoulders, it was somehow wrapped several times around his neck, getting tighter. Instead of fur he felt scales. He looked to his right, where the head of the nis would always lie purring. It appeared to be changing. Like a strobe light that flashes, one second it would be the nis he always knew and the next second be a creature he had never seen before. Beady eyes, a split tongue flipping in and out of a scaly mouth, and somewhere to his left, rattles. Then back again to the soft, warm, furry, black and white pet that he loved and added so much to his life.

"Charley," hissed the creature. "It's over. It's time to take you home."

"What is happening?" Charley moaned in terror. "The nis is my friend, my companion, my strength. It is so small, so soft, so gentle, so delighting, so invigorating. How could it be changing into something ugly? How could it have taken over my life, my relationships, my work, my everything?"

"Oh, I've not changed," hissed the creature. "You're seeing what I've been all along. Now I am fully in control. It's time for me to take you to the other side. Nothing can help you, you are mine!"

"NOOOO!" Charley screamed in confusion. "Someone, anyone help me! Isn't there anyone who can rescue me?"

The Decision

At that moment the front door burst open. Calmly an unassuming man, dressed in white, walked in surrounded by a group of people also dressed in white. Gently, but firmly, he said, "Charley, this creature has been ruling your life for a long time and you didn't even realize it. You've been unwilling to see it? Do you realize it now?"

"Yes," said Charley meekly.

"Charley, I can rescue you, free you from this creature. But more than rescue you, I offer to treat you as a son, provide for you, make your life what you were created to be. Look at these people with me, they are free and you can be like them. Do you want that?"

"Yes," choked Charley, the pressure increasing around his neck.

"Charley, listen carefully. If I rescue you, you must surrender your life to me forever. No more playing with this or any nis. Are you willing to do so?"

"I guess so," Charley mumbled, more focused on the nis than the man's words.

"*NO!* Charley, look at me. You must make a deliberate choice to serve me. Will you?"

"Yes, but I don't see how I can do that." Several of the folks in white walked to Charley, put their arms around him. "We didn't think we could do it either, but it is possible. Just surrender. And we'll help you."

"Charley, one more thing," continued the man in white. "You must be willing to allow me to destroy this creature."

Charley balked. He remembered all the times they had together, back in the early days when it was small, and soft, and made Charley feel so good. Maybe it would be that way some day again. Surely it wasn't as bad as it looked right now. Maybe it was just having a bad day, or maybe it was sick. We could have those good times again, couldn't we? Charley vacillated even as the nis squeezed tighter and tighter.

"Charley, look at your nis. Hear the rattles. Feel the hiss. It is evil. It does not love you. It has deceived you all these years, waiting to control your life and eventually murder you. There is nothing good in it. It only wants to destroy you, now and forever."

The man in white waved his hands over Charley's eyes. As he did, something like rose colored contacts fell from his eyes. Charley looked, saw the nis, really saw it, for the first time saw it. He saw the ugliness, felt its grip around his throat, smelled the stench of its scaly body. As the light of understanding came on, Charley realized that the nis was moments away from killing him.

"Charley, you must hate this thing and surrender yourself to me."

"I do," he cried.

"Charley, the nis must die. I know you are unable to kill it. That is why I'm here. I only need your pledge to me and your permission and I will kill it."

"Yes, yes, I surrender. Save me."

The Rescue

With those words still hanging in the air, the man in white grabbed the creature with amazing strength and lifted it from Charley's neck. Oh, the freedom in that moment. Freedom he had not experienced in, well, forever. He felt safe and loved and lighthearted and giddy and so many things that he couldn't describe. What wonder!

Part Four: Holy and Holding

In the exhilaration of rescue he had almost forgotten about the man in white. Finally Charley glanced to the right to see the man lifting the snake. For a moment it appeared he would dash it to the ground. Instead, he draped the creature around his own neck. Without resistance the creature wrapped itself around him, choking, squeezing. The man dropped to the floor in agony, yet did not resist. The creature continued to squeeze until there was no more life. Charley was in shock. How could this be? The man was so strong. He saved Charley, he could have saved himself. Fear began to grip him again. With the man dead, surely the creature would return to do the same to him.

Frozen, Charley could only watch. The nis did not move. In fact, it could not. It was as if the murder of the man by the nis had also taken its life. Both lay still.

As he stared at the man and creature in an awful heap, he noticed for the first time in years the letters on the side of the animal. The letters long ago pointed out by the youth in the circle. They were different. From this angle, with the light of understanding, in the freedom granted Charley by the man's sacrifice he realized that the letters were not "N, I, S", at all. Rather, they were "S, I, N." Sin. It was not a nis, but a sin that had lured him, manipulated him, controlled him and nearly destroyed him. The man in white had taken Charley's sin, wrestled it, and died to set him free.

Still staring, suddenly the man in white sat up, threw off the sin, and smiled at Charley with a love deeper than anything Charley had ever felt. Scars from the attack circled the man's neck. "Deadly, nasty, horrible creatures, those sins. But not deadly, nasty or horrible enough to destroy the Son of God or those who surrender to Him. Now, let's get on with the good life I have for you." With that He put His arm around Charley's neck and gently guided him away. When his Savior's arm touched Charley's shoulders, a strange thing happened. Warmth radiated into Charley's neck, across his shoulders, down his arms and legs. But instead of lulling him toward twilight, it filled him with a keen awareness of life and reality. In that moment Charley realized that the warmth of the nis/sin was a counterfeit of what he was experiencing now.

Every day, Charley sees the creatures. Every day, Charley hears the whisper of invitation again. Sometimes another type of nis, often the same breed as his. Sometimes the whisper is nearly overwhelming. But when he looks up, into the face of his Savior, the power comes to walk away from the invitation and into the warmth He provides. Much to the anger of the creatures.

> We know that our old self was crucified with him in order that the body of sin might be brought to nothing, so that we would no longer be enslaved to sin. -- Romans 6:6
>
> Therefore, since we are surrounded by so great a cloud of witnesses, let us also lay aside every weight, and sin which clings so closely, and let us run with endurance the race that is set before us, -- Hebrews 12:1
>
> Let not sin therefore reign in your mortal body, to make you obey its passions. Do not present your members to sin as instruments for unrighteousness, but present yourselves to God as those who have been brought from death to life, and your members to God as instruments for righteousness. For sin will have no dominion over you, since you are not under law but under grace.
> -- Romans 6:12–14

Lord, invite me into your safe loving arms. Onto your lap.

God is neither male or female. He is both + more. He has all the loving warmth we connect to mothers. Yet he is strong and leads us to safety like a father. Both genders are made in his image then he must be a combination of both. Plus, he is the Almighty creator, the precious lamb who died for us, and the Holy Spirit who dwells in us. Altogether, a majesty we spirit cannot comprehend. He is man and woman, holy God in the trinity. And available to all.

PART FIVE

"On" Is Way Different Than "With"

Part Five: "On" is Way Different than "With"

CHAPTER NINETEEN

NOT JUST "WITH" GOD

To sit on God's lap is so much more than sitting beside Him

Sitting *with* God is great.

But it is way different from sitting *on* God's lap.

I had been **around** God all my life. Being around God meant I was in the vicinity of God, but was not personally connected. I was around God when my mom read me Bible stories and taught me prayers and when I attended Sunday school. But being around God is way different than being with God.

When I was fifteen years old, I began to be **with** God. Being with God meant I was connected in relationship. I accepted the invitation to a personal relationship with God and started to take Him seriously. Through the influence of godly people, church worship, youth group activities, personal prayer and Bible study, I was with God and the relationship grew. It was good, but it was not enough for God. Or for me, though I didn't realize it at the time. Being *with* God is way different than being *on* God's lap. And on God's lap is the place we all long to be, the place of true satisfaction.

A Job I Didn't Apply For

I did not apply for the job. Did not send my resume and did not interview. In fact, I didn't even know there was an opening. It just happened. But there is no question that I am the official, sanctioned and approved, executive "Opener and Distributor of String Cheese" – at least for our grandson, Brodie.

The boy loves, loves, loves cheese. One day, with ten month-old Brodie in one arm, I pulled a shrink wrapped package of string cheese from the fridge. The boy about flung himself out of my arm. We sat down on the couch as he impatiently watched me unwrap the snack and break it into bite-sized pieces. As he learned to toddle, Grandma would give him string cheese and say, "Take it to Grandpa." On wobbly legs, Brodie would bring it to me, and I would open it and break it into bite-sized pieces. At sixteen months, he now pulls the refrigerator door open (when Grandma allows), grabs string cheese, and, with a monumental smile while holding it up like the Olympic torch, runs to me. It doesn't occur to him that the other adults in the vicinity could open it. That's just fine with me. I've got the only union card in the house.

More importantly, there's the issue of seating. As he reaches me, Brodie raises his arms in the silent demand to be put in my lap. Because that's where you sit when you eat string cheese. At least when you're under five years old.

Even better, if I happen to be on the floor crossed legged, this little Olympic String Cheese Sprinter will hurry to me, hand me the cheese, stop, turn his back to me, take two steps rearward and flop down into my lap. Stop and get a good mental photo of that. Without asking permission, paying attention to what I am doing or with regard to my wishes, Brodie stops, turns his back, steps back two paces, and drops into my lap. Authoritatively. Audaciously. Then contentedly sits, sometimes even blissfully leaning his head into my chest, as I hand him his bite size pieces of the tasty treat. Because, you see, I am the official, sanctioned and approved, executive "Opener and Distributor of String Cheese."

And it is a privilege to serve that role. I'm happier than Brodie and I don't even get cheese.

I find it interesting that Brodie does not consider, does not pause, does not hesitate to land in my lap. He does seek my okay, does not consider my feelings or entertain the possibility that I might get angry. He just plops into my lap. Why?

Because he knows he *belongs* there. Because he likes it there. Because he feels loved there. Because he is comfortable there. Because He intuitively understands that he is valued and safe there. Thus, there is no fear – only confidence that my lap is the right place to be. In fact, he acts like he owns my lap, using it for any purpose at any time.

And…He's right. It is pure delight to have him on my lap, which makes no logical sense. I'm a busy guy and always have more on my to-do list than I can get done. Yet I *make* time for this knee biter. I'm not accomplishing a task, finishing a project, selling a book or completing a talk. I'm sitting on the floor handing bits of dairy product to a toddler, which appears to be to be work for me and benefit for him. Yet I get greater enjoyment from the on-the-floor moments than from any of the tangible tasks. I *look forward* to being with him, and secretly hope there are times when he will sit with me even though it may seem to be a waste of valuable time. Rather than a waste, it is an investment because I was created to love and be loved, to give of myself to those I love, and to do life with others. So were you.

Is God Like That?

That all sounds good, but is it the right picture of God's relationship with us – almighty, perfect God with imperfect people?

The idea of sitting *with* God, (the theme of my first book, "From Where God Sits"), is comfortably appealing. It's safe, more under our control, less intimate. But sitting with God is way different from sitting *on* God's lap. You sit with a friend, maybe even close. When you are with someone, you may touch shoulders, pat a back, slap hands, or give a teasing shove. But sitting *on* a lap is one of the most intimate things a person can do.

When the boy arrived to great fanfare, he had no choice but to be on my lap. Now he does. I could have told him when he learned to sit, "Brodie, the time has come for you to sit with me instead of on my lap." But I didn't, because *on* is way different than *with*. There is closeness when he is on my lap. Sure, I could put my arm around him while he sat with me on the couch, but it's not the same. There is acceptance on my lap. There is safety, a depth of relationship, and closeness on my lap. None of which is deeply experienced if Brodie is only with me. It's still good, but incomplete – for both of us. Because *on* is way different than *with*.

Thus, it is essential to answer the question, "Is sitting *on* His lap genuinely the picture God wants all of us to have?" Before we answer that one, let's look at it from the other side.

Where does our love for kids come from if it is not a reflection of His love for us? Where does our desire to be close to our kids, to hold a child in our arms, to rock a fussy baby or to eat string cheese with a toddler come from if it is not a reflection of God's desires with us?

Unless God is our loving Heavenly Dad inviting us onto His lap, how could we do so?

Maybe the question is not so much, "Is sitting on God's lap an accurate picture?" but "How can God *not* be like that if we, imperfect human beings as poor reflections of God, are like that with our kids?"

I believe the *only* reason this Grandpa can love as I do is because God first loved me as the Bible clearly states.

> There is no fear in love, but perfect love casts out fear…We love because he first loved us.   -- 1 John 4:18a–19

So is Brodie sitting on Grandpa's lap a good picture of God with us? **Nope.** It is the right picture, but a fuzzy one. It is an inadequate, poor picture of the right image dimly reflecting the relationship God desires with us. It is an inadequate, poor picture because God's love is so much bigger and His desire for us to be *on* His lap is so much stronger than the best of human relationships. Though inadequate, it gives us the truth that *on* His loving, holy, perfect lap is *exactly* where God wants us to be. Being *with* God is good, but it is not where God wants us to be.

Sitting on His lap is genuinely the picture God wants all of us to have of Him.

As a Grandpa delights in his grandson dropping onto his lap, God delights even more. God's heart for us is far bigger than my heart for Brodie.

Being on God's lap is not just for special people, but for all people. My delight for my granddaughters, Cadence and Maddie, being on my lap is just as strong as for Brodie.

We absolutely should boldly and audaciously act like we belong on God's lap, that it is ours because God has invited us there.

How do we get there? Repeated experience has taught Brodie that on my lap is where he belongs. It's the same with us. It took me six months to take even a tentative step towards God's lap. I pray you are faster. Take some tentative first steps towards that deeper relationship. Listen for God's voice through the Bible and prayer and respond. God will do the heavy lifting to get you on His lap if you will lean towards Him, let go of all that holds you back and hold your arms out for Him to lift you up.

Part Five: "On" is Way Different than "With"

CHAPTER TWENTY

"MERRY" OR "MIGHTY" CHRISTMAS?

To sit on God's lap makes us see common things in His uncommon way

There's much sword rattling about the physical display and verbalizing of the phrase "Merry Christmas" these days. It's getting into conversations in a lot of places.

But have you ever stopped to ask yourself what "***Merry*** Christmas" is all about? Fact is, it's bothered me over the years and since everyone else is talking about it, now might be the time to lay it out there.

Is it akin to "Robin Hood and his *merry* men"? What kind of a description for thieves, however noble, is that? Were they really jolly? Was it that they drank so much Nottingham apple beer that they were artificially happy? Did they laugh a lot? That sounds more like the "Men in Tights" version of the movie than the brave warrior in the Kevin Costner film. Do you really want to wish others a "***tipsy*** Christmas?" I don't think so.

Or is it, like, merry is like, really giddy and like, giggly and like, the stereotype of like, valley girls? You know, like, scattered? (My apologies to all those wonderful, intelligent valley girls out there.) Is that *merry*? Do you really want to wish others, like a "GIGGLY Christmas?" Like, I don't think so.

Maybe it means hanging enough lights on your house to illuminate the city of Pittsburgh? Is it to highlight Frosty in full costume? Is it to mount genuine deer hide reindeer on your roof with a Santa that waves and chuckles? Is it the glitz and glitter and entertainment and (I'm not kidding -- this is a real song) "I Want a Hippopotamus for Christmas?" Do you really want to wish others a "***superficial*** Christmas?" I don't think so.

If not, what is this *merry* Christmas business all about?

On an episode of the radio program, *Family Life Today*, the host, Dennis Rainey, invited writer Ace Collins to help the audience understand some of the background of Christmas songs and traditions. Ace explained that the phrase "*merry* Christmas" goes back over 500 years to old

England. As with so many words, the meaning has changed from its original use. Rather than happy, merry meant "mighty" – powerful, grand, strong. Thus, the Christmas phrase was much more than a nice greeting; it was a desire for others to have a *mighty* experience of Christ's birth. Robin's men may have been happy, but being merry meant they were strong, powerful men. To me, that makes a whole lot more sense.

Mr. Collins goes on to explain in his book, "Stories Behind the Best Loved Songs of Christmas,"[6] that the song, "God Rest Ye, Merry Gentlemen" has a far deeper meaning than first glance indicates. "Rest" did not mean to sit around in the recliner watching Steelers football. Rather, it meant "to make." In addition, the comma was not originally between ye and merry, but between merry and gentlemen. Hmmmm, changes everything. With that restoration in hand, what we have is, "God Make You Mighty, Gentlemen." Whoa! A far cry from, "I hope Santa makes you giddy!"

Think of the implications.

Instead of singing "We Wish You a Merry Christmas", it will be "We Wish You a *Mighty* Christmas."

Pretty much destroys "Have Yourself a Merry Little Christmas" when instead of hoping people have a quaint, wonderful holiday we intend for them to encounter a powerful experience. *Mighty* and little just don't seem to stick to one another.

At the end of that best loved Christmas poem – you know the one where your wife is wearing a kerchief and you're wearing a cap in bed (what is a kerchief and why in the world would I be wearing a hat in bed?) – the part where Santa flies off into the sky and yells to the sleeping town below now becomes "*Mighty* Christmas to all and to all a good night."

As Ebenezer Scrooge is, well, scrooging through Christmas Eve, I wonder if he could have avoided the three ghosts if Bob Cratchet had wished him a *Mighty* Christmas. You know, he's the kind of guy who just might respond to that.

Guys may be more willing to shop and decorate if they had to rise to the challenge of a *Mighty* Christmas! Maybe it's the subconscious idea of merry/giddy/jolly that deters us.

And, of all adjectives, the One who came that first Christmas is perhaps described best by *Mighty*. Mild as a child, but *Mighty* as the man--

Part Five: "On" is Way Different than "With"

God. Humble, yes. Loving, yes. Kind, yes. Holy, yes. But encompassing all the characteristics of Jesus, He is MIGHTY!!!

So when your next Christmas comes around, join me in starting a new movement. Instead of the standard "Merry Christmas," let's wish others "*Mighty* Christmas!" That's sure to turn a few heads! It might even create some opportunities to talk about the good news of God coming to earth – which is the most important activity of every Christmas season for those who personally know Him.

So, let me be the first to wish you a ***mighty, powerful, bold*** celebration of the God of the universe coming to earth to rescue us!! *God WITH us!* and *Mighty Christmas!*

> Finally, be strong in the Lord and in the strength of his might.
> -- Ephesians 6:10

> For this reason I remind you to fan into flame the gift of God, which is in you through the laying on of my hands, for God gave us a spirit not of fear but of power and love and self-control. Therefore do not be ashamed of the testimony about our Lord, nor of me his prisoner, but share in suffering for the gospel by the power of God, who saved us and called us to a holy calling, not because of our works but because of his own purpose and grace, which he gave us in Christ Jesus before the ages began
> -- 2 Timothy 1:6–9

CHAPTER TWENTY-ONE

I KNOW YOUR HURT

To sit on God's lap allows God to help us when we hurt

The first thing a child does when he gets hurt is to look around. He looks around for a parent, grandparent, or caregiver to run to for comfort, care and assurance, one who will dry his tears. When our children were younger, some days they would return home from school, look for Sheila or me and burst out bawling. He fell and scraped his knee. She was ignored by her friends. He was insulted. She was unfairly corrected by a teacher.

What they needed most was not a solution to their problems. It was to be enveloped in some big arms and to hear, "***I know...***I know it hurts. I know what you're going through. I know it is unfair. I know it makes you feel sad, alone, different."

Eventually they needed answers, but they did not need answers first or most. Oh, they would need to talk it through later and get direction to go forward, but in the moment of tears they needed someone to identify with their feelings and emotionally respond. They needed to know that someone bigger, who loved them dearly, could assure them it would be okay. They needed to know they were not alone. They needed to know someone else recognized and acknowledged their hurt and hurt with them. They needed to know that someone would be with them all the way through it. They needed to hear, "***I know...***"

That is one of the reasons Jesus tells us to become little children. As God's dearly loved children who face hurt, we can experience the same care and hope-giving assurance. "***I know...,***" God says as we sit on His lap. If we "act like adults," pretending that life does not hurt, the pain bottles up until it boils out in anger and depression. The truth is, with our loving Heavenly Dad, we *are* little kids in grown up bodies with the same needs as our kids. We can try to deny it, but God created us that way.

> ...'Truly, I say to you, unless you turn and become like children, you will never enter the kingdom of heaven.'
> -- Matthew 18:3

Part Five: "On" is Way Different than "With"

Around 95 AD, the Christians in the church at Smyrna were going through incredible pain. They had been persecuted, their property confiscated or destroyed, slandered for their loyalty to Jesus, facing more pain and possibly death, feeling like they were less than others. They were coming into the house of God hurt and confused. What did they need? Not answers. They needed to hear *"I know..."* from someone bigger who dearly loved them, could identify with their pain and could assure them it would be okay. Someone who could let them know they were not alone and would be with them all the way through. They needed to hear, *"I know..."*

In the letter from Heaven that Jesus dictated to the Apostle John, He did exactly that.

> I know your tribulation and your poverty (but you are rich) and the slander of those who say that they are Jews and are not, but are a synagogue of Satan. -- Revelation 2:9

Jesus wraps His arms around His dearly loved children and tells them *"I know..."*

We all get hurt. Life delivers pain to us with frustrating regularity. No one is exempt. What you need, what I need, during those times is not answers right away, though eventually we will need direction so we can go forward. We need to sit on God's lap, feel His strong, reassuring arms around us and hear, *"I know...*I know it hurts. I know what you're going through. I know it is unfair. I know it makes you feel sad, alone, different."

Just as Jesus did for the Christ followers in the city of Smyrna 1,900 years ago, He will do for us when we run to Him. Most often, He will do so through other children as He uses the flesh and blood arms of another person. Sometimes, we sit on His lap and hear His voice through the Bible, prayer and worship. But you can be confident as you run home to Him that He will be there – arms outstretched, tears in His eyes as you weep, holding you tight and whispering, *"I know...I know..."*

CHAPTER TWENTY-TWO

SOMETIMES YOU NEED SOMEONE

To sit on God's lap means we sit there together, finding the remedy for aloneness

There's something to be said for just being together "with" another person. Being together in a way that somehow, someway, is life infusing.

Some days I just *want* someone to be "with" me. It's not that I'm in need, I just like company. It's not a necessity, it's a bonus.

Other days I *need* someone to be "with" me. Bad news, heavy circumstances, empty tank, not sure which way to turn or some other tough stuff causes me to really, really *need* someone. Sometimes I need that person for help, answers, or advice, but often I simply need another person's presence. When it is a need, it's not a bonus, it is an unqualified necessity.

We were created to "be with," to share life together – the ups, downs and ordinaries. It is impossible for human beings to not need others. We are incapable of going it alone and surviving emotionally, if not physically, which explains much about hermits and recluses. Our very nature requires doing life "with" others.

I confess I struggle to wrap my mind around this because it makes no logical sense. On a purely intellectual level, the emotions we feel, the actions we take, and the sacrifices we make in our relationships don't compute. Yet, when we shift the lens to include the heart, it makes more sense than nearly anything else towards which we put effort.

My favorite name for God comes from the Christmas story. Immanuel, "God *with* us." The birth of Jesus is all about God coming to earth to meet the "*being with*" need we have in our relationship with Him.

> "Behold, the virgin shall conceive and bear a son, and they shall call his name Immanuel" (which means "God with us").
> -- Matthew 1:23

Christmas was only the beginning. God knew that we would never, could never, know Him and His ways unless He came to be Immanuel,

Part Five: "On" is Way Different than "With"

"God *with* us." Jesus being *with* mankind in human form allows us to actually see a bit of who He is, what He wants to do, how He loves us, what life is really all about, how to enjoy relationships and so much more. Without God *with* us, we are stumbling and fumbling.

The *being with* need is broader than our relationship with God. In His immeasurable wisdom, He created us with the need to be *with* other people in addition to being with Him. Because He knows it is best.

> Then the Lord God said, "It is not good that the man should be alone;
> -- Genesis 2:18a

It is not unfortunate; it is *bad* for a person to be alone. Aloneness is the source of many of peoples' struggles – struggles that could be resolved if they had someone to be *with* them.

> Bear one another's burdens, and so fulfill the law of Christ.
> -- Galatians 6:2

We are to be *with* one another to share burden carrying. Someone has said that our burdens are doubled when carried alone and halved when shared with others. That is a wise person.

> Two are better than one, because they have a good reward for their toil. For if they fall, one will lift up his fellow. But woe to him who is alone when he falls and has not another to lift him up!
> -- Ecclesiastes 4:9–10

> Rejoice with those who rejoice, weep with those who weep.
> -- Romans 12:15

Being *with* means we enter into other peoples' lives, that we do life together, sharing in the joys and sharing in the sorrows.

The wonder and power of the day when God came to be *with* us can be lost. On Christmas morning, children run to a synthetic evergreen draped with imitation lights and man-made décor to rip away artificially colored paper from manufactured boxes, believing the metal/plastic/wood/particle board items inside will make them happy. Then they lay them aside sooner or later for another item they hope will make them happy. Again and again. If they only focus on the stuff, they miss the gift that will truly satisfy – the presence of people they care about and the love that is possible.

As we grow up, we don't do that anymore, do we? Hmm...yeah, we do. Every day, people look to man-made, artificial, manufactured possessions, experiences, and relationships believing those will make them happy. Focused on what can be seen, they miss the unseen gift that will truly satisfy – God *with* us and people *with* us.

Let's agree together that we will refuse to run after plastic counterfeits to be *with God and others.*

PART SIX

We Lost It All and Need it Back

Part Six: We Lost It All and Need It Back

CHAPTER TWENTY-THREE

THE ENORMITY OF WHAT WE LOST

To sit on God's lap is to begin to make our way back home

Once upon a time, there was a world filled with creatures and empty of humans. And there was a God whose nature is love, but had no being to return His love. Oh, Father, Son and Holy Spirit were in perfect community, holy relationship among the Persons of the Trinity, but God had a desire to pour out His love with abandon to a creature with a free will. So after doing a marvelous job of creating a perfect world, God created a man who was a reflection of Himself with the ability to think rationally, steward creation for God, but most of all, with the ability and desire to live in love relationships with God and people.

So from the moment God put the finishing touches on the dirt and Adam emerged, it was perfect relationships all around. With God and all of creation. Hear me now: **Perfect!!** From the beginning, it was God's plan to create for Adam a mate. In fact, God gave Adam the task of naming all the animals with the ulterior motive of causing Adam to notice that every other creature had a mate. When in perfect relationship, God creates both desire and the fulfillment of that desire. So God hit Adam with the anesthesia and performed surgery and a miracle. Surgery to remove Adam's rib as the base material and a miracle to make a woman from the rib. As Adam wakes up, Eve comes to life – a perfectly matched pair, the ideal couple.

Everything God has done was because of God's nature of love and was perfect. Adam and Eve had a perfect existence – perfect relationship with God, with all of creation and with one another. Nothing to hide and nothing to protect themselves from, so there was no need for clothes. They had an intimate relationship with God, who would visit in some form every day, in perfect harmony so that fear didn't exist on earth. God gave them meaningful work to do that was a perfect joy. Not only was there no fear, there was no worry or exhaustion or sickness or death or sadness or hurt or frustration or loneliness or anger or pride or conflict or discouragement or criticism or laziness or diets or suffering or being too hot or too cold or…you get the idea. ***Perfect.***

It is the story of love all the way around. Until…yeah, you know the story. Eve ate of the forbidden fruit and then Adam joined the banned banquet. Their minds' eyes were opened and they realized they were naked. Hiding replaced transparent acceptance. When God came calling, the blame game replaced honesty and responsibility. Their disobedience destroyed the perfection of all creation and opened a Pandora's Box of evil that permeates everything from that point forward. Death entered as God killed one of the animals Adam had named and one of their sons murdered his brother.

I don't think we can ever fully grasp all that was lost because we have no real point of reference. Often, the description of this initial sin is contained to breaking God's direct command that changed man's relationship with God. Sometimes the description includes the riff it caused between the first man and first woman. Stopping there leaves us with a superficial concept. Because we cannot comprehend perfection, we cannot grasp the enormity of what was lost.

Also lost was man's understanding of God and the relationship He desires. It's not so much that a command was disobeyed as a relationship was betrayed in the breaking of that command. There's been a hole in our souls ever since that only God can fill. It is an ache that cannot be ignored. But because we are blind to the fact that it is God-shaped, we chase after pleasures, possessions and position, believing those will sate the longing. We can't help it. It is a longing so strong that it literally drives us to find a way to fill it.

The saddest of all ripples of the tragedy in the Garden is that we've lost the knowledge that it is relationship with God that satisfies. Most people have an inkling that there is a God and that we have some kind of responsibility with Him. Some people know that we are to have relationship with Him. Of those, there are some who understand God is love and Jesus died to provide a way for us to have a relationship with Him. But very few truly believe and have experienced the kind of intimate relationship God originally designed us for and still wants with us, even after all the pain we've inflicted on Him.

Part Six: We Lost It All and Need It Back

That is where the picture of sitting on God's lap comes in. That is the kind of relationship the human species has been longing to get back ever since the original man and woman stepped out of Eden. The devil does all he can to keep us blind and away from it, even as God marshals all of Heaven's resources to make it happen. It's time we said "yes" and crawled up on our loving Heavenly Daddy's lap. He's waiting and longing and hoping. Because that is who He is.

> therefore the Lord God sent him out from the garden of Eden to work the ground from which he was taken. He drove out the man, and at the east of the garden of Eden he placed the cherubim and a flaming sword that turned every way to guard the way to the tree of life.   -- Genesis 3:23–24

> remember that you were at that time separated from Christ, alienated from the commonwealth of Israel and strangers to the covenants of promise, having no hope and without God in the world. But now in Christ Jesus you who once were far off have been brought near by the blood of Christ.
>   -- Ephesians 2:12–13

The blood of Christ brings me near to Papa God. It bought and paid for my cleanliness. I am now worth to climb into his lap.

CHAPTER TWENTY-FOUR

I WANT MY HEART BACK!

To sit on God's lap leads to reclaiming our hearts

It has been a lifetime crusade for Inigo Montoya in the movie Princess Bride[7], this search for the man with six fingers on his right hand. He explains that this man commissioned Inigo's father to craft a special sword that took a year to make. The six-fingered man came back, demanded the sword at 1/10 the promised price, then killed his father when he refused. The eleven year-old Inigo loved his father and challenged the six-fingered man to a duel. The man spared him, but left scars on both cheeks of Inigo's face. "When I was strong enough, I dedicated my life to the study of fencing. So the next time we meet, I will not fail. I will go up to the six-fingered man and say 'Hello, my name is Inigo Montoya. You killed my father, prepare to die.'...It's been twenty years and I'm starting to lose confidence."

Later in the film, the six-fingered man turns up as Count Tyrone Rugen, evil right-hand man to the king. Finally coming face to face with his father's murderer, Inigo chases him through the king's castle. As Inigo rounds a corner, his enemy throws a dagger into Inigo's stomach. He gasps, falls against a wall and whispers, "Sorry, Father. I tried. I tried."

His adversary mocks, "You must be that little Spanish brat I taught a lesson to all those years ago. Simply incredible. You've been chasing me your whole life only to fail now. I think that's the worst thing I've ever heard. ***How marvelous!***"

Inigo pulls the dagger out as he attempts to stand. "Good heavens! Are you still trying to win?" jeers Count Rugen as he walks toward Inigo and thrusts his sword. Inigo has just enough strength to block the attack and step forward. "Hello, my name is Inigo Montoya. You killed my father, prepare to die" he mumbles as he falls against a table.

Again the Count attacks. Inigo begins to walk haltingly forward as he protects himself against a second sword thrust. "Hello, my name is Inigo Montoya. You killed my father, prepare to die."

Part Six: We Lost It All and Need It Back

Count Rugen nervously attacks again as Inigo defends himself with a bit more strength. Gaining strength with every step forward, his passion returns. *"Hello, my name is Inigo Montoya. You killed my father, prepare to die."*

"Stop saying that!" barks the six fingered count as Inigo backs him against a table. Inigo stabs each shoulder and the man knows he's in trouble.

Inigo moves from defense to offense and shouts, ***"Hello, my name is Inigo Montoya. You killed my father, prepare to die!"*** Inigo slashes the man's left cheek.

"Offer me money."

"Yes!"

"Power, too. Promise me that." Inigo slashes the man's right cheek.

"All that I have and more." Then Count Rugen begs, "Please."

"Offer me everything I ask for."

"Anything you want!"

In one last attempt to defend himself, the cowardly count raises his sword to swing. Inigo grabs his hand, delivers the death thrust, and with faces inches apart says, "I want my father back." Inigo drops him to the floor, dead, justice achieved for his father.

After reading John Eldredge's book, *Waking the Dead*[8], I was praying while walking on my treadmill when God brought the above scene to my mind. Then my soul surprised me.

From somewhere very deep inside me came this cry...

"I want my heart back!!"

Just as Count Rugen stole what Inigo valued most, satan has stolen our hearts through the battle in Eden. Where God created purity, satan put sin. Where God created peace, satan put fear. Where God created joy, satan put sorrow. Where God created contentment, satan puts dissatisfaction. And worst of all, where God created love, satan puts mis-directed, self-focused desire.

With more fervor than Inigo, I want my heart back! I want every corner cleared and free. I want to live and love with passion. I want to be free to be all God created me to be.

I believe that is the cry of every heart – *your* heart. The heart-cry of the human race.

Problem is that early on our enemy begins to steal our hearts. Through temptations, hurts, disappointments, lack of love, false love, lost love, abuse, condemnation, legalism, unreasonable expectations, and on and on the list of his methods go. Satan steals a corner here, a corner there. Until we either lose heart or build such a wall around it that we no longer function "with heart" at all. We just function.

This is not about feelings or emotions; it's about the real you. Your heart is who you really are. It is the place of motives, desires, creativity, courage, commitment and dreams. It is the location of conscience, imagination and deepest thinking. Emotions are simply the results of the real you coming to the surface. Your heart is where God gives life. When we give into temptation, we give satan pieces of our hearts. When we are hurt by others, satan tries to get us to hide our hearts. The end result is that we live "without heart", without the fullness of life Jesus came to give us. That He still offers to all of us.

Perhaps you are thinking, "But I'm a Christian, so my heart is already back." Not quite. There is a difference between forgiveness and reclaiming our hearts. Forgiveness cleanses us of the guilt of sin. Reclaiming our hearts only comes when we allow Jesus to kick the devil's counterfeits out, to destroy the strongholds he created, and to fill those emptied places with the Holy Spirit. In doing so, Jesus transforms our core being into His image and we are free to live in step with Him. Intimacy and freedom.

Inigo was not a murderer; he was a man with a little boy's heart still stinging from the loss of his dad.

We are not bad people; we're children in adult bodies who still sting from the loss of our heart until we snatch it back and give it to God.

Inigo refused everything, all the offers of Count Rugen. His request for money, power, and everything he wanted was only made to show that there was nothing of value that could make up for the loss of his father.

When we realize there is nothing of greater value than heart intimacy with God, we will begin to reclaim our hearts.

Just as the six-fingered man mocked our hero, telling him how marvelous it was that Inigo was going to fail, that he wasn't good enough,

Part Six: We Lost It All and Need It Back

and that he was a loser, so our enemy attempts to convince us of the same lies.

Just as Inigo refused to believe the lies to live truth, so must we. Clinging to God's truth, we can live life "with heart," being what we were created to be and accomplishing what God created us to do. The devil will be defeated and his lies shattered.

How about you? Do you want your heart back? It doesn't come easy; you will have to fight for it with the power of God. Start today – tell satan, "I want my heart back!" Tell God, "I give my heart back to You, do whatever You want." It is the first step on the journey to recovering your heart. A journey that ends in sweet victory.

> Above all else, guard your heart, for it is the wellspring of life.
> -- Proverbs 4:23

> So we do not lose heart. Though our outer self is wasting away, our inner self is being renewed day by day.
> -- 2 Corinthians 4:16

I start the journey, having reclaimed my heart from Satan and given it to God. Lead me to love as you love. Teach me to be kind as you are kind. Nourish my faith, giver of faith.

CHAPTER TWENTY-FIVE

WHAT DID WE EXPECT?

To sit on God's lap causes us to learn and live God's absolutes

The world is shocked, appalled, devastated, surprised, and disappointed by the many discoveries of corporate fraud motivated by greed. But what did we expect?

The older generation looks at the lack of morals and values of so many in the younger generation and wonders what the world will be like in a couple of decades. But what did we expect?

Those who enjoy sports cannot believe that millionaires who get to play baseball for a living would even consider going on strike. But what did we expect?

The entertainment industry is constantly pushing the envelope on what is allowable in TV, movies and music until it appears most is unfit for human consumption. But what did we expect?

And those of us who are striving to present the message of hope and love in Christ struggle to find many who are interested in the depths of what God offers. But what did we expect?

A society that has no sense of absolutes is bound to experience the harvest of that deficiency. Harvesting is funny that way. We reap what we sow. Period.

A little history. In the fifties, the music industry pushed on the boundaries of absolutes and found them to be softening. Elvis and some of his contemporaries didn't seem too harmful and so we said, "Okay."

In the sixties, the prosperity of the post world war economy, the "if it feels good, do it" attitude and the questioning of moral absolutes, came together in an unparalleled rebelliousness in America. Everything was up for grabs. Christians were thrown backwards by the sheer blatant disregard of it all. The root of relativism was planted and selfishness became king. Moral absolutes were abandoned as prayer was taken out of school, the Ten Commandments no longer mattered, and relativism replaced religion.

The seventies were a continuation of the sixties without the riots. Instead, a steady revolution continued to undermine right and wrong. The eighties and nineties saw the kids from the sixties take positions of corporate and governmental power. They had not changed except that now they wore ties instead of tie-dyed T-shirts. Though they possessed position, they had not returned to the absolutes they abandoned decades before. Instead of a plumb line of right and wrong to guide them, they pursued a path of selfishness, rule bending and relativism. It simmered underneath the surface until it surfaced to rule the culture. The moral vacuum continues to be exposed as corruption continually hits the national and international spotlight.

But what did we expect? That a society without absolutes would somehow find its way to honesty, integrity, character and fairness to all? Now we've reaped what we've sown. Corruption, self-serving actions, destruction of thousands of retirement benefits, and favoritism have rippled throughout the world. Decency standards in entertainment have been worn away and the industry is influencing folks to lower standards even further and further.

But what did we expect? The only sure way to reap anything different is to reestablish absolutes.

> The one who sows to please his sinful nature, from that nature will reap destruction; the one who sows to please the Spirit, from the Spirit will reap eternal life. Let us not become weary in doing good, for at the proper time we will reap a harvest if we do not give up.   -- Galatians 6:8--9

There must be some standard to hold us strong when the tests and temptations of life come. Otherwise everything is up for grabs. But absolutes are of little value unless they are founded on something that is absolute. Where do we turn? Remember those Ten Commandments that were once displayed in every school classroom? That's a start. From there, we can open up the rest of the Bible, God's authoritative truth, and discover the absolutes to live by in every situation.

That works for us as individuals, but how can we influence an entire nation or world that has lost its way? Beware: one of Satan's schemes is to overwhelm us with the enormity of the problem so that we raise the white flag of defeat, pull back into Christian organizational bunkers to protect ourselves and keep a safe distance from the "people out there."

That was not Jesus' way while on earth, nor is it His plan for us. As we look to Him, we can be bearers of hope as we love as Jesus loved and live as Jesus lived. If we choose to consistently, persistently live out God's ways, we will influence others for God, touching one person at a time. A return to God and His absolutes will not happen by mandate, but by individuals and groups of people living lives of love by God's standards, in His power, for His purposes. We will not see an immediate difference. We may not even see much in our lifetime. But we dare not stand idly by, throwing rocks at the lack of morality in frustration. Rather, we must *be* the light that shines the way to God, *be* the salt that brings the flavor of Christ and *be* the aroma that spreads the fragrance of Christ everywhere we go.

Then what can we expect? That we will be at least one group of people who desire God and strive to live by His standards. And who knows where the ripples of that might go! *Never underestimate the power of God working through those who love Him.*

Let's do it! One day at a time. One person at a time. One situation at a time. One decision at a time. From the smallest, seemingly insignificant moment to the monumental, obviously important. One at a time.

> He told them another parable: 'The kingdom of heaven is like a mustard seed, which a man took and planted in his field. Though it is the smallest of all your seeds, yet when it grows, it is the largest of garden plants and becomes a tree, so that the birds of the air come and perch in its branches.' He told them still another parable: 'The kingdom of heaven is like yeast that a woman took and mixed into a large amount of flour until it worked all through the dough.' -- Matthew 13:31-33

CHAPTER TWENTY-SIX

DON'T FEED THE ANIMAL

To sit on God's lap causes us to nurture the things that make us more like Jesus

Don't feed the animal.

I guess my mind was open enough for the enlightening and weighty thought to pop into my head as I stood in the shower. Not new, but powerful when applied to some of what I've recently observed. Beautiful in its simplicity and complexity.

Don't feed the animal.

If I don't want the stray kitten to hang around, grow, become attached and impossible to excommunicate – *Don't feed the animal.* Easy to grasp, not so easy to execute when you like the ball of fur.

The reason you and I struggle with thoughts, behaviors, habits, emotions and more is because we are feeding the animal! By the time I stepped out of the shower it occurred to me that we are being dense. We don't have to struggle so hard in so many ways if we will *stop* feeding the animal!

Jesus walked the earth showing us the way. Though fully God, He was fully human and faced the same choices we face – which animals to feed. The reason He lived aligned with the Father, full of abundant life, purpose and contentment, was because He chose to feed the right animals. Our lives can have the qualities Jesus enjoyed as we make the same choices He made.

If I don't want negative thoughts to hang around, grow, control my mind and become impossible to excommunicate – don't feed the animal.

If I don't want harmful habits to hang around, grow, control my actions and become impossible to excommunicate – don't feed the animal.

If I don't want hurt and anger to hang around, grow, consume my heart and be impossible to excommunicate – don't feed the animal.

If I don't want temptations to hang around, grow, overwhelm me and be impossible to excommunicate – don't feed the animal.

If I don't want negativity to hang around, grow, hold me hostage and be impossible to excommunicate – don't feed the animal.

On the flip side, what do we see Jesus "feeding?" On the flip side, *do* feed the animals you want to hang around, grow, benefit you and be impossible to excommunicate…

… right thoughts
… good habits
… forgiveness, love, patience
… obedience to Christ
… victory over temptations
… positivity
… and kittens if you want them.

Reflect for a moment. Over the past week, what animals have you fed? You can identify them by noticing what is hanging around in your mind and heart. That which stays is what you give nourishment. That which leaves is what gets starved.

We can be like Jesus, experiencing life as He did as we change our feeding habits. Which animal will you feed today?

> Do not be deceived: God is not mocked, for whatever one sows, that will he also reap. -- Galatians 6:7

If I don't want to feed negativity – don't waste time on FB. Choose wisely what to watch. Start some new books.

CHAPTER TWENTY-SEVEN

WHEN TRAGEDY STRIKES, DO THIS FIRST

To sit on God's lap means our first response is to Him

My heart ached as my friend told me about yet another tragic mass shooting. What a waste! What unimaginable sadness for the families! What a heartrending irony! And it has become commonplace.

I awoke to more details of the appalling attack and the efforts of so many to do *something, anything* in response. To want to do something is a natural response. It is difficult to be helpless and useless, but most of us are too far removed to do anything about such nightmares.

That kind of frustration is one significant reason these situations hit us so hard. Frustration because we feel powerless as we hear the hour by hour details of an attack and those struck down. Frustration because it makes us feel vulnerable. Frustration because these things are not supposed to happen. Frustration because we want to do *something, anything* to help others and provide an outlet for what we feel inside.

We *can* do something meaningful! It may not be the action you would most like or even feel is worthwhile. Quite often it has been relegated to last place. Many, if not most, people hear it as a cop out or perceive it as a religious nicety. Some don't think of it as action, don't believe that it will make any difference, or is merely something to do when you can't do anything else. If we hold those beliefs, taking this action will not always relieve our frustration. Yet, it has proven to be a most powerful force.

We *can* do something that makes a difference. When we make it our first response instead of our last. When we understand it as essential instead of optional. When we make it our automatic, knee-jerk first-aid response instead of an afterthought. When we embrace that it is the most powerful thing to do instead of a placebo. *Then* we will make a big difference, no matter the distance or the enormity of the tragedy.

PRAY

What we can do

What is it?

Pray. Yes, pray.

It is *the* most powerful action we can take. Not because of us, but because it connects us with the holy Almighty God of the universe who transcends time and distance. We should fully embrace, sincerely believe and actively practice it as *the* thing to do first, last and in between. It is the action that transforms us from helpless, useless, powerless, vulnerable and frustrated to helpful, useful, powerful, invincible and at peace.

If you have trouble believing that it is most powerful, will you accept that it is more powerful than being glued to the news, wringing your hands and feeling awful?

Praying while sitting on God's lap is especially powerful. If you struggle to pray, start by joining God on His throne as His dearly loved child.

This was the way of Jesus. Before He began His public ministry, He pulled away for forty days – and emerged full of the power of the Holy Spirit. Routinely, He made time to be with the Father for strength and direction. And He powerfully received it. Before going to the cross, Jesus first went to the Father in the Garden of Gethsemane. God provided the supernatural physical, emotional and spiritual strength that Jesus required to endure the tragedy of the cross.

What will we do?

If someone recorded our immediate reactions to life's ups and downs, would there be a lot of film used on things we do before we pray or would it be the first thing recorded? Would they conclude that prayer is something we do when we can't do anything else or that it is *the* action to take to access the greatest power in all creation?

I challenge you to make prayer your first response to everything. To go to God for the good and the bad, the wonderful and tragic.

I challenge you not to pray when all else fails, but pray first so that all else doesn't have a chance to fail.

I challenge you not to pray when there's nothing else to do, but pray first so we will know what to do.

I challenge you to pray believing that connecting with God mysteriously moves His hand and also simultaneously transforms us.

I challenge you to pray anywhere, anytime, with anyone and for any reason.

The results of that kind of prayer are powerful beyond comprehension.

The earnest prayer of a righteous person has great power and produces wonderful results.   -- James 5:16 (NLT)

When we act first, we often do things that are not helpful and can make matters worse. When we pray first, it leads to actions that make a difference. Pray first, act second and both will be effective and powerful.

Let's pray first. Let's be most powerful.

PART SEVEN

Don't Just Sit There

CHAPTER TWENTY-EIGHT

THE FIRST OF MANY STEPS

To sit on God's lap launches us toward all that is good

God's lap is where it begins, but not where it ends. It is a picture of regaining what we lost in Eden. As we sit there, two wonders of this relationship open up: intimacy and alignment.

The more we know Him, the more we will love Him – intimacy. Out of that close relationship, we will understand all that God does and commands is out of pure love; He desires what is best for us and others.

The more we love Him, the more we will obey Him – alignment. We will seek out and live His will. Not as a duty, but as an expression of love and confidence. Obedience to our loving Heavenly Dad is our path to love and life that satisfies.

God has been working to get you on His lap all your life, but also to give you a life of confidence, love and power.

An American Parable

The child was born in the usual way. Tiny, helpless, cute, wonderful. When he was put on his mother's lap or when pulled into his father's arms, he stayed there. Not like he had a choice. The grandparents, aunts, uncles, cousins, neighbors and friends celebrated his birth, oohed and aahed and made the strange sounds only a baby can extract from perfectly adult adults. Everyone wanted a chance to hold him because laps and arms are where babies belong. And all was right with the world.

At the family reunion six months later, grandparents, aunts, uncles and cousins greeted the child with the requisite, "My, how he has grown" comments along with more strange sounds, making the child wonder what kind of family he had been born into. The relatives were again thrilled to see the child. Even more so to hold him because laps and arms are where babies belong. And all was right with the world.

Twelve years and six months later, the grandparents, aunts, uncles, cousins, neighbors and friends gathered for the boy's thirteenth birthday. Because his family lived on the other side of the world, the boy had not seen nor been seen by the gathered adults. They clustered around the cake and the child puzzled. The oohs and aahs were replaced with hmms and wows. Being polite people, no one asked but all wondered, "Why was the thirteen year old always sitting on his parents' laps?" All had been glad to see him, but had no desire to hold the five foot three inch boy because laps and arms are most certainly not where teenagers belong. All was no longer right with the world.

Grandparents, aunts, uncles, cousins, neighbors and friends felt awkward but obligated to attend the boy's high school graduation party. Now six feet tall and 250 pounds, rumors had it that the boy was home schooled because he cried when he wasn't on his parents' laps. And he had no plans to leave home for college, tech school or a job for the same reason. Now the sounds from the adults were whispers, tsk's, my-my-my-my-mys accompanied by shaking heads. All was very wrong with the world. Finally, the newest cousin, whether brave or simply honest, asked, "Why's that boy sitting on his mom's lap? He's bigger than she is!"

The group let out a collective gasp, being polite people, and tried to shush the youngest member of the clan. The faces of the boy's mom and dad turned a noticeable pink with managed anger. "Young one, this is where our son belongs." And to the collection of adults, "You all were in favor of the child sitting on our laps. What is the problem now? This is where he belongs."

"No," said the wise grandfather. "When the boy was a baby, his place was on the laps and in the arms of those he trusted. But as a child grows, he must also help around the house, go to school, learn how to be an adult. He must learn to add value to the world as you help him discover the gifts and abilities God gave him to live productively in this world. He can't just sit there. He has to live!!"

I hope you realized by now that the story is a parable. Let's call it, "The Parable of the Average American Christian."

Just as a child cannot remain a child, but must progress to value-adding adulthood, so we cannot always be on God's lap. There is a time and a place to sit as little children on God's lap. But there is also a time and place to be adults doing what God tells us to do. God's lap is to be a launching pad from which we live with Him and for Him. Regularly, God's lap is to be the place we connect with God, receive direction and perspective on life, gain the strength to face difficulties and overcome temptation, accept correction and discipline, obtain healing and enjoy relationship with God. But then, we launch!

The Sequel

I arrived a day early with several of the other staff coaches for the SCORRE[9] workshop in Denver, Colorado in May of 2000. We decided to worship with a Hispanic congregation whose pastor was a friend. Since it was the Sunday before Cinco de Mayo, this celebration of a victory in Mexico's history was masterfully used as a picture of our victory in Christ. We could sense God's presence.

As the worship service closed with communion, I sat in my seat, cup and bread in hand, bowed my head and God showed up. Again. With the same picture of God on the throne inviting me to sit on His lap. In my mind's eye, I quickly accepted His invitation and, with tears once again streaming down my face, experienced the unbridled joy that only God can give.

Out of nowhere it changed. Past experiences led me to expect that I would stay on God's lap for a while, then open my eyes at the end of the service. Instead, before I was ready, the picture in my mind changed to God lifting me off of His lap, setting me down, and turning me to face away from Him. Standing there I saw myself being filled with the Holy Spirit and I heard God's voice say, "Go, do my work."

I confess that, for a moment, I was upset. I felt blindsided. For a couple years, I had been experiencing the breathtaking affirmation of being on God's lap and now God was changing it. And it didn't feel very nice.

I like being on God's lap for all the reasons I've written about. It is comfortable, soothing, safe, and full of happiness. I had not struggled for six months to get onto His lap just to be put down again, had I? Actually, I had no idea what I had signed up for. The invitation was to sit on His lap, but evidently there was much more to it. I'm glad to say the moment of confusion passed quickly as the familiar joy of being filled with God's Presence brought tears. And it made sense. There is a time to sit on God's lap and a time to do what He tells us to do.

It was the way of Jesus. Over and over and over Jesus pulled away from the crowds to be with the Father. Being fully human as well as fully divine, He had to reconnect to gain direction and power (sit on God's lap) to do the Father's work. Then He went back to the work the Father sent Him to do.

As God showed me when I worshipped in Denver, there is a time to sit on God's lap and a time to be on our feet doing God's work. A time for intimacy in relationship and a time for alignment in obedient service. A time to get filled up and a time to pour ourselves out. It's a pattern to build into our lives: sit on God's lap, on our feet, sit on God's lap, on our feet.

It is the best way to live, and boy is it living!

> So also faith by itself, if it does not have works, is dead.
> -- James 2:17

> Look carefully then how you walk, not as unwise but as wise, making the best use of the time, because the days are evil. Therefore do not be foolish, but understand what the will of the Lord is.
> -- Ephesian 5:15-17

Part Seven: Don't Just Sit There

CHAPTER TWENTY-NINE

LIVING FOR THE DOT OR THE LINE[10]

To sit on God's lap is to live for what lasts

Imagine you and I are standing together in my backyard. I have a roll of three-inch wide paper wound around a stake in my hand. I ask you to drive the stake into the ground, which you do with finesse and strength. A helicopter descends, a passenger reaches out, takes hold of the paper, flies north, carefully unwinding the three-inch roll of paper. At 25 miles, it reaches the end of the roll (it's a big roll), lands, and the passenger attaches his end of the paper to another stake and drives it into the ground.

We begin to walk along the roll to see that it contains the history of time. We see the story of Adam, Eve, the serpent and the expulsion from the Garden. Cain and Abel. Abraham, Isaac, Jacob, Moses leading the exodus from Egypt, Joshua conquering the Promised Land, Elijah, Elisha, Isaiah. The kingdoms of Babylon, Greece, Rome. David killing giants and writing songs, Solomon exercising wisdom and his seven hundred weddings, the enslavement of Israel for disobedience. As we walk, we come to the story of Jesus' earthly life – Christmas, His temptation, miracles, death, resurrection and the gift of His Presence through the Holy Spirit.

We continue on to see the early Church continue the work of Jesus, Christianity turning the world upside-down even through persecution after persecution. The acceptance of Christianity by Caesar Constantine, the fall of the Roman Empire, the Middle Ages, the sad irony of the Crusades, the Dark Ages, the Enlightenment, the American Revolution, Abraham Lincoln and the Civil War, the Industrial Revolution, two World Wars, Vietnam conflict, the Civil Rights Movement, the embarrassing hairstyles and clothes of the seventies, the upheaval of the eighties and nineties, September 11. We finally pause, after many miles of history, at the present day.

You look carefully for your own life, (as we always do, trying to find ourselves in a picture), but can't quite make it out. I hand you a very powerful magnifying glass, with which you finally see your name and birth date. After checking for a date of death (sorry, it's not there), you look closer to see the symbol representing your life – a dot. "A dot!" you roar, "My life is only a dot! All the time and energy I put into living on this rock, and it's only a dot!"

Yeah, a dot. In the scheme of history, you and I are only a dot, a spot, a pencil mark, a speck, an instant, a moment, a mark on the long march of time. Perspective is humbling.

Only a dot, but we are dots on the long line of time. A dot in the context of all that is before and all that will be. A line is defined as "a straight one-dimensional figure having no thickness and extending infinitely in both directions."[11]

The words that catch my eye in that definition is the phrase "extending infinitely in both directions." Standing on our dot looking backwards, we can see the line extending forever – not the line of human history, but of God's existence. Looking forward, we see the same, but with a change. Somewhere ahead, the line fades into a vast, golden carpet that leads to a mansion beyond anything the lives of the "rich and famous" have ever imagined. At the door stands the Savior Himself, with open arms. Catch the picture? You are an almost invisible mark on the history of time, yet a God created and valued part of the eternity.

All of which begs the question Randy Alcorn poses[12], are we living for the dot or the line? And another, *should* we be living for the dot or the line? I think the answer to the second question is easy; it is a simple matter of mathematics. The answer to the first is harder, challenging us to surrender what we can see, touch, taste and feel, for what is mostly unseen but is more real. In the scheme of history and eternity, the dot will quickly be over; the line will last forever.

Living for the dot of earthly existence or for the line of eternity is a choice we make every day. Most days, however, we don't even recognize we are making it. Which will you live for today?

> What good will it be for a man if he gains the whole world, yet forfeits his soul? Or what can a man give in exchange for his soul?   -- Matthew 16:24--26 (NIV)

CHAPTER THIRTY

YOU MIGHT BE SELFISH IF…

To sit on God's lap is to let Him fill us with His love for others

Human nature tells us that happiness comes from personally pursuing that which makes us happy. Jesus tells us that a life that is satisfying, meaningful, purposeful, and love-filled comes from pursuing Him.

There is a *big* difference between pursuing happiness and life. Jesus said,

'I came so they can have real and eternal life, more and better life than they ever dreamed of.'   -- John 10:10b (The Message)

Abundant life. Life to the full. Life that is satisfying.

But the world is upside down. And we experience the opposite.

According to Jesus, experiencing the satisfying life is in direct proportion to how much we live upside down from typical selfishness. We do so when we…

>give up being self-focused and become other-focused
>give up selfish choices to make selfless selections
>give up gathering for ourselves to instead provide for others.

It's a tough sell and an even tougher way to live because the hundreds of messages that bombard daily tell us to grab, get, push, climb, win. To live out Jesus' words and example is to paddle upstream, against a Mississippi-like current. Either the world is upside down or Jesus is upside down.

That's why, when we see the runner at a Special Olympics event choose to lose a race by stopping to help another participant, it touches something deep inside us. Even veteran, hardened reporters tear up. The satisfying life chord is struck when the world is turned on its head and Jesus' ways and values pop right side up. Even if it's just for a minute.

Wouldn't it be wonderful if a lot of life was filled with the music of that satisfying chord? To do so requires that we identify where self-focus still rules in us, surrender it and allow God to transform us into other-focused people.

Intimacy and Awe: Walking with the Real God

Most people would not admit to being selfish. We can always find someone with whom to compare ourselves who makes us look good. It makes us feel bad to admit selfishness. We know it's ugly, so we soothe our consciences periodically. Another reason we don't admit selfishness is because we may be blind to its subtle forms. In fact, it's possible to serve other people in ways to make us feel good rather than truly meeting the needs of others.

To help us with our natural blindness, I came up with a checklist. Feel free to add to it. You might be selfish if:

you get angry when someone cuts you off.
you refuse to forgive.
you don't allow yourself to be inconvenienced.
you are not generous to the point where you feel it.
you are unhappy.
you refuse to help certain people.
you are lazy.
you think that your agenda is more important than that of others.
you insist on having your way.
you always have to win or be right.
you refuse to sincerely apologize.
you insist on being in control and find it hard to compromise.
you hear constructive criticism as a personal attack.
you don't give back to God what is His.
you find it difficult for someone else to be the focus of attention.
you don't want to work with others on a team.
you choose events for your benefit rather than to help others.
you usually give negative feedback first.
you are irritated when others ask you for help.
you hear a sermon and think "_____ (fill in a name)" should hear it.
you think, "someone should do something about this" rather than doing it yourself.
you are self-conscious about being seen with certain people in public.
you are grumpy, sour and complaining.
you only help others when it makes you feel good.

Part Seven: Don't Just Sit There

I'm not pointing fingers or trying to guilt you. But if you identified with any of the above, you should feel a sting of conviction. It's just that I *want* you to experience the satisfying life that only comes when we are other-focused, the level of which is in direct proportion to your selflessness.

Or as God puts it...

> give, and it will be given to you. Good measure, pressed down, shaken together, running over, will be put into your lap. For with the measure you use it will be measured back to you.
> -- Luke 6:38

CHAPTER THIRTY-ONE

WORTHSHIP THAT IS TRUE

To sit on God's lap is to give Him His proper place

You blink. Instead of standing in your driveway, you are on a dusty road. Instead of sweater and slacks, you are in a robe. Instead of shoes, sandals. Instead of a briefcase, a palm branch. Hundreds of people are crowding the street around you. A cacophony of sound wafts toward you from just beyond view. Children squeal, women sing, men shout. Not sure if the mob is mad or happy, you step into the doorway of the closest building.

The surge of sound moves closer. Conversations, exclamations, hurried calls to "come see" turn into shouts of admiration and unprompted singing. The source of commotion finally comes into view. Seated on a donkey is a man, thirty something, riding slowly through the dusty streets. Men spontaneously design something of a makeshift carpet, laying their outer robes and tree branches on the roadway before him. Women and children wave palm branches in salute. Ah, that's why your briefcase disappeared and a palm branch is clutched in your hand. All close by join the chorus being repeated, known to everyone but you, "Hosanna! Blessed is he who comes in the name of the Lord! Blessed is the King of Israel!"

"Must be the king of the country," you whisper under your breath.

"Not yet," replies the man next to you. "But we hope he soon will not only be king of Israel, but the one who frees us from Romans as well."

You watch as the object of all the attention rides by. Doesn't look like a king. Seems awfully ordinary, much like any man in the crowd. You shake your head at the whole affair. Never in your life have you experienced such enormity of emotion from an assembly. Not only in what you hear, but what you can feel. Looks as if the entire city is shouting, singing, waving branches.

Then He looks at you, the one on the donkey everyone is here for. Not a passing glance, as one stranger to another, but a knowing look as if He has known you forever and expects you to know Him too. His gaze seizes your soul, drawing you toward His as time stands still. Ordinary on the outside, He becomes extraordinary with that strangely wonderful stare. With no logical explanation, you now comprehend the reason for the excitement; He is more than a man. You could not explain it under oath, but you are convinced.

Having caught the excitement and power racing through the crowd, you are convinced He will be crowned king, whether those in power like it or not. The air is magnetic, pulling you into the momentousness of it all. Even you, a stranger from another time and place, can see the rightness of the parade. You wave the branch and shout the praise.

Palm Sunday. Surely, of all the days that ever were, that was a day of true worship. A day when Jesus was given praise and honor that was long overdue him. When God was recognized as God. We even call it, "The Triumphal Entry." But things are not always as they appear.

Fast forward a few days. Same city, but the powerful intensity of the throngs has changed from love to anger. Instead of praise for His life, the crowds shout for Jesus' death. The one they claimed as king, they refuse to allow to be released. The one they exalted, they mock as He is beaten. The one they believed would free them, they demand be bound and confined. The one who was the subject of their songs, has become the accused they murder on a cross. Had so much changed? Had Jesus done something to go from hero to goat that moved Him from deserving the highest praise to deserving the cruelest death?

The problem was not with Jesus, but with the expectations of the people on that Palm Sunday. They were praising him, worshipping him, honoring him because they thought he would give them what they wanted. For hundreds of years, the Roman Empire had cruelly occupied Israel and the Israelites desperately wanted freedom. ***That's*** what they expected Jesus to give them. He didn't. Though He could have easily done so, He blatantly refused. Squashed expectations make the people mad. Especially when we feel they are legitimate expectations, when we feel promises have been made. When things did not go the way they wanted, the crowds turned their backs on Jesus and their leaders killed Him. Their desires blinded them from truth…and what they needed most.

That's the way with expectations. Often, they don't define what is best for us and others, or what we need most, or what we actually want in the depths of our hearts. In missing who Jesus came to be, the crowds missed what they longed for most. They exchanged God's greatest offer to pursue an invention of their own imaginations.

We're not like that, are we?

We praise Jesus, honor Him, sing to Him, profess our undying loyalty to Him. Why? Because He deserves it, right? We'd like to believe that is true, but too many times it is not true in our hearts. It behooves us to take a closer look. It is possible that instead of worship simply because Jesus deserves it, we offer it because we believe that God will give us what we want in return? That we sing because it makes us feel good? That we pray because we want something, even fast when really serious? That we give money because we think God will give it back multiplied?

What are we thinking? Same thing the crowds were thinking so many years ago. Human nature doesn't change.

So it goes…"Oh, God, save me from this mess and I'll serve you forever!" Or "heal me, correct my mistakes, let me pass this course, or (fill in the blank) and I'll give You first place for the rest of my life!"

That's not worship, that's called "let's make a deal." Then when God doesn't do what we want because He knows it is not best, we bail out on Him just like the Israelites.

(In fact, sometimes we bail even when God *does* what we ask, but that's a different issue.)

Worship is not a way to get what we want from God.

The concept of worship is rooted in the idea of "worthship"–honoring God because He is God, and, as the one, true, Almighty God, He is worthy of it. Period. No strings attached. It is making God #1 in our lives, everything we do and say. One form is activity commonly done in a church worship service: singing, praying, communion and studying the Bible with others. But it is far from confined to that. The bigger form is living our entire lives in ways that honor and please God.

True worship is expressing "worthship" by our actions, words, attitudes, thoughts, relationships, work, play…you get the idea. Giving "worthship" is motivated by the truth that God is God and deserves complete control of our lives. No deals, no if-thens, no requiring God to hold up His end of some contract we manufacture and He never signed. It is loyalty to God no matter what.

Had the Israelites worshipped Jesus that way, they would have turned the city upside down with praise on Easter Sunday after God did the work He intended all along. When God did what was best for all. When God offered what they actually wanted and needed. But NOOOO, they bailed when things didn't turn out their way. And lost the greatest moment of all.

One of the best pictures of true praise comes from an unlikely source, Job. Not job, as in where you work. Job, the guy famous for all his problems; the man behind the phrase, "the trials of Job." His fame actually ought to for what he did during and after all the trouble for which he is known. We ought to recognize him for his worship. Listen to his words…

> Though he slay me, yet will I hope in him;
> -- Job 13:15a

That is true worthship. In the middle of the trash heap of life, when there was nothing else that could go wrong, Job still honored God as God. He expresses his total loyalty to God and then backs it up with his life. Even after his wife told him to give up.

> Then his wife said to him, 'Do you still hold fast your integrity? Curse God and die.' But he said to her, 'You speak as one of the foolish women would speak. Shall we receive good from God, and shall we not receive evil?' In all this Job did not sin with his lips.
> -- Job 2:9–10

Would we do that?

Let's express our worship well when we gather. But even more, let us live our lives to "worthship" well. As people look at our lives, let there be a fluorescent arrow pointing them to God.

> In the same way, let your light shine before others, so that they may see your good works and give glory to your Father who is in heaven.
> -- Matthew 5:16

CHAPTER THIRTY-TWO

STORMS

*To sit on God's lap does not make life easy, but it is **THE** place to be when storms come*

Storms are those times when the waves crash over us and the winds threaten to blow us overboard, never to be seen or heard from again.

They come in many forms, but one thing is for sure – *everybody* goes through storms! Financial storms. Relational storms. Physical health storms. Emotional storms.

Sometimes they are predictable, but more often they catch us by surprise, even when we are working hard to stay close to Jesus. It's not an accident – sometimes it is Jesus who lands us in the storm. Not because He abandons us, but because He loves us.

Hard is not Bad; Hard is Hard

We tend to think of storms as bad. Storms are definitely hard, but not necessarily bad. Hard is not bad – hard is hard. No question storms are painful, but they don't have to destroy us. In fact, storms give us unique opportunities to experience what is impossible during the calm.

It is in the storm that fluff and bluster is blown away and what is really real remains. In the storm, we see what is bigger…what is most powerful. Or should I say "Who."

When Jesus sent his disciples into the storm (Mark 4), He was deliberately sending them into a situation that would challenge their previous understanding of power. He slept while his followers struggled to row toward shore, all the while hanging on for dear life in the teeth of a monsoon. Finally, they shook Him awake, scolding Him for not caring about them. He calmed the storm and asked them, "What is your problem?" (my interpretation). He questioned them about their lack of belief in Him. Their response? Slack-jawed terror. They were petrified that the One they followed had power over the storm. *Disoriented* by the whole ordeal, they had to think things through in a brand new way.

Part Seven: Don't Just Sit There

How Many Storms Does It Take?

Some time later Jesus did it again, but this time He sent the disciples ahead without Him. (Matthew 14). For this experience, He intentionally positioned the disciples in the middle of a lake during a hurricane where sure drowning loomed in their immediate future. Jesus put them there by design so they would once again struggle in fear. This kind of helplessness and disorientation was the only way for them to realize they were powerless and see that He was all powerful. You're not ready to see God's power until your power is gone. At the point when they believed they were going down, Jesus walked on the surface of the lake toward them. Their off-the-chart adrenalin levels led them to believe He was a ghost until He revealed Himself. At the end of themselves, they were willing to metaphorically crawl onto God's lap. Jesus stepped across the waves to calm the storm on the sea and in the disciples' souls. Once again, the storm allowed them to experience that Jesus was truly God. Storms will do that...if we crawl onto God's lap.

Mark Batterson contends that Jesus must *disorient* us so He can *reorient* us. I agree. Jesus must force us into circumstances that get us "out of whack" so that He can align us with what is true. The disciples believed that the devil controlled the sea; Jesus had to show them that He did. The disciples believed the storm was going to kill them – twice; Jesus had to show them nothing could even hurt them unless He allowed it. The disciples believed that Jesus did not care about them; Jesus had to show them that it was because He *did* care that they ended up in the middle of the fiercest storm.

The truth is that every storm we go through on God's lap is a gift to make us strong for future storms. Every time we come through one, having been disoriented enough to be reoriented to Jesus' truth, we are more capable to handle an even bigger storm. And, believe me, they *will* come. If we never battled through storms to discover that we can survive and thrive in God's strength, the mildest wind would destroy us.

So let's not bemoan the storms that come, let's look for the reorientation that is a gift from Jesus.

> On that day, when evening had come, he said to them, 'Let us go across to the other side.' And leaving the crowd, they took him

with them in the boat, just as he was. And other boats were with him. And a great windstorm arose, and the waves were breaking into the boat, so that the boat was already filling. But he was in the stern, asleep on the cushion. And they woke him and said to him, 'Teacher, do you not care that we are perishing?' And he awoke and rebuked the wind and said to the sea, 'Peace! Be still!' And the wind ceased, and there was a great calm. He said to them, 'Why are you so afraid? Have you still no faith?' And they were filled with great fear and said to one another, 'Who then is this, that even the wind and the sea obey him?'
-- Mark 4:35–41

Immediately he made the disciples get into the boat and go before him to the other side, while he dismissed the crowds. And after he had dismissed the crowds, he went up on the mountain by himself to pray. When evening came, he was there alone, but the boat by this time was a long way from the land, beaten by the waves, for the wind was against them. And in the fourth watch of the night he came to them, walking on the sea. But when the disciples saw him walking on the sea, they were terrified, and said, 'It is a ghost!' and they cried out in fear. But immediately Jesus spoke to them, saying, 'Take heart; it is I. Do not be afraid.'
-- Matthew 14:22–27

PART EIGHT

Never Ending, Ever Changing

CHAPTER THIRTY-THREE

IT'S THE START

To sit on God's lap sets the trajectory for the life we want

It is tempting to think that the day in 1998 when I finally got on God's lap was the moment of I planted a flag at the top of a mountain. Victory! We made it! Trophy lifted and streamers drifting on my head. And all was good for life. But that is not true. Please read the following statement several times. Slowly. Let it sink in.

Crawling up on God's lap was the beginning.

A very, very good beginning, mind you. An important beginning that sets everything in motion as birth is the beginning for a child and parents. A time to celebrate, to shed some tears, to treasure the wonder of the experience. It is the beginning of the incredible life with God He so longs for us to have. Crawling up on God's lap was a watershed moment, a turning point that changed everything and set the trajectory for the rest of life. For all who choose to say "Yes" to God's invitation to Daddy-child intimacy, it is the wonderful beginning of a life long journey of getting to know God more, deeper, better. There's a lot unleashed when you start sitting on God's lap regularly.

It's the Start of Seeing God as He Really Is

Too many to count are the times when a dearly loved child is on the lap or in the arms of a parent. Every time the child is there, a connection is made, something meaningful is transferred, the bond is strengthened. It a gift from God that human babies are some of the most helpless creatures on earth. That vulnerability causes the parent to give his/her heart to the child and causes the child to really know the parent.

A young man stood in a sterile room as his wife lay on a bed. Also in the room were professionals who would help add another being to the human race. After months of anticipation and hours of true labor, the doctor announced, "It's a girl!" to the thrill of all in the room. Except for the child.

Intimacy and Awe: Walking with the Real God

Cadence, a seven pound, fourteen ounce girl, had made her grand entrance into the lives of my son, Chadd, and his wife, Liz. And she was not happy about it.

"What in the world is going on?" I imagine her thinking. "I was doing just fine in my warm, comfortable, dark home complete with feeding tube. And all of a sudden somebody starts pushing and squeezing me through a way too narrow tunnel, forcing me toward who knows where. After all that, it's all loud and bright and cold and scary. And what's with all the poking and prodding and rubbing? Whose idea was this, anyway? I think I'll just wail for the rest of my life."

And boy did she wail!

At first it was all smiles, laughter, and congratulations among the adults. "Boy, what a set of lungs," quipped one, stating the very obvious. Ear-piercing cries continued as the staff made sure her airway was clear and breathing was good. "She'll settle down as soon as we wrap her in this warm blanket," assured one experienced delivery room expert.

She didn't settle as the verbal storm increased a few decibels.

Concern began to replace smiles as Cadence's screams echoed off the walls. "She's healthy. I don't know why she is still crying so hard. Usually they settle down by now."

And she continued to wail.

"Let me hold her," said her daddy. They placed the child into Chadd's arms; he turned her to face him, pulled her close so her face was inches from his own and looked at his just arrived daughter with love.

And she wailed even more.

Quietly, Chadd's deep voice began fill the room. *"You are my sunshine, my only sunshine,"* he began to sing. A song he had sung to her during the months of anticipation.

Then it happened. Like the flip of a switch, the snap of fingers, the blink of an eye. By the time Chadd reached the second phrase, the child went quiet. Not a gradual wind down of wailing. It was instantaneous halt. The screaming that had perforated eardrums a split second before simply, suddenly, immediately stopped as Cadence's eyes peered into her daddy's.

"You make me happy when skies are gray." Not only was Cadence silent, so was every adult as they froze to watch the unfolding miracle of love.

"You'll never know dear how much I love you." Tears formed in every eye privileged to watch this sacred moment.

"Please don't take my sunshine away." Quiet. Except for the sniffles. And the hushed words, "I've never seen anything like that in all my years as a doctor," to which every medical professional nodded agreement. "Nothing like that…ever," as no one wanted to move. Sacred moments will do that. Who wants to leave a miracle, after all?

What happened? A scared child, held tightly in her daddy's arms, close to her daddy's heart, heard her daddy's voice and immediately knew all was well. Everything that had caused Cadence to be so full of fear was trumped when she felt the love and heard the voice of her daddy.

I have tears in my eyes as I write this story over a year later. Perhaps you do as well. I hope so. Because that tender love touches our souls as a reflection of our Heavenly Daddy and our longing to feel His love and hear His voice.

It's the Start of Experiencing God in So Many Ways

One of Jesus' primary purposes when He walked the earth in human form was to give mankind the true view of God. As we see Jesus' actions and hear Jesus' words in the Gospel accounts, we can get a more and more accurate picture of God *if we will do so sitting on God's lap*.

There are many reasons for a child to be on the lap or in the arms of a parent. When God first invited me to sit on His lap, it was like a parent cradling a child only minutes in the world. It was about affirmation, expressing value, peeling away lies, setting me free. Over the years, I've come to understand that there are a load of purposes for being on God's lap. Sometimes we choose to climb up on His lap while other times He reaches out to pull us there. Initially, we will only be on God's lap when we choose, but once we establish the relationship we will at times find ourselves being hauled into His lap kicking and screaming for our highest good. Just like a loving parent does when the child doesn't know what he/she needs.

In truth, the picture of being on God's lap is a metaphor for every experience of deep connection between God and one of His dearly loved children. The chapters in the different sections of this book have been stories of a variety of those experiences. Below is a sample list of God's purposes for being on His lap. As you read through the list, jot down your own experiences as they come to mind, then flip through the chapters of this book to see where yours connect with those I've written about.

Relationship. The pleasure of being together with no agenda. Simply enjoying the friendship by being together. *In the tree-top In early AM + PM in bed. In nature Singing*

Protection. We are not strong enough to handle every situation. Sometimes we need God's protection, just like a toddler needs her daddy's strong arms around her. *Depression, Wreck, Duodenal perforation*

Assurance. The peace and confidence that everything will be okay, especially when fear threatens to overwhelm us. *Tim's Cancer, Wreck of family*

Correction. Being shown where we're going wrong and how to correct it while God holds us close and guides us true. *New house neighbors*

Teaching. Times when we need God to show us how to stretch, grow and work hard to become what He created us to be and do. *Covid lockdown*

Conversation. Being on God's lap is simply a great way to have serious talks or friendly chats. *AM & PM*

Part Eight: Never Ending, Ever Changing

Waiting. When something is supposed to happen and it has not yet, God's big arms provide patience and certainty in an uncertain world.

When tired or waking up. I love holding my grandkids as they drift off or awaken. It's a great place for the child and a joy for me. It's the same with God. *[Love this]*

To get places. Sometimes, to get where we're going we need God to carry us. Just like a two foot tall toddler moving in an adult world, sometimes we need Someone bigger to carry us. *[In hospital]*

To see better. The higher up, the better the vantage point. As it is with little ones living in a world of kneecaps, so it with us. *[Wisdom]*

To feel better. Life *will* wear us out, make us sick, get us grumpy, hurt us. It is then we need to be on God's lap for healing, comfort, strength. Interestingly, often we need it most when we seem to want it least.

Therefore, my beloved, as you have always obeyed, so now, not only as in my presence but much more in my absence, work out your own salvation with fear and trembling, for it is God who works in you, both to will and to work for his good pleasure.
-- Philippians 2:12–13

Not that I have already obtained this or am already perfect, but I press on to make it my own, because Christ Jesus has made me his own. Brothers, I do not consider that I have made it my own. But one thing I do: forgetting what lies behind and straining forward to what lies ahead, I press on toward the goal for the prize of the upward call of God in Christ Jesus.
-- Philippians 3:12–14

CHAPTER THIRTY-FOUR

THERE JUST AREN'T ENOUGH HUGS

To sit on God's lap lets God walk us through both the joy and pain of loving and living with people

No matter how many years you share with a person you love, you will want more. No matter how much time you have with people you love, it is never enough. And no matter how many times you embrace a person you love deeply, it will never, ever, ever, ever be enough. It is simply impossible to fill up your heart.

In the back of my mind I knew this truth, but it's all fiction and fairy tales until you go through it. I was willing to face it, but I'm a bit miffed it had to come as a monstrous locomotive. It slammed into me the day we sent our oldest to college. (Read: when I had my soul torn apart by letting my kids grow up, become adults and move away from home).

Sent the first one off and was ready for some sadness but I was completely taken aback by the antics of my heart. In my head I knew it was right, he was in God's place for him, he was ready and it was all good. Yet my heart was in full-scale mutiny, "Noooooooo. Don't let him go, bring him back, spin the clock in reverse, hold him tight, protect him and never let him go" it screamed at me. I've never had such a civil war within. "Let him go – hold on to him - let him go - hold onto him…" Dropped him off in central Indiana. About 2 hours into the 8-hour drive home, my heart won and I sobbed like a baby.

With emotion blurring rationality, I kept thinking, "If I only had a little more, I wouldn't feel this way." I wished I had spent more time, done more things, had more conversations about the important issues of life, taught more skills, and on and on and on. And, most of all, I kept wishing I'd **hugged him more.** Then I would be okay with him now out of hugging range. Ironically, my son now tells me I did enough of all those things (perhaps even too many of some). But in driving away, I felt my heart split with the finality of the moment and the desire for more.

Part Eight: Never Ending, Ever Changing

So I vowed I would do more with the remaining three children so that I would not feel this way when we revisited this big moment in their lives. And I did. Probably to their annoyance.

But my heart had lied. The next one went off to school and still there were not enough hugs. I sobbed and wanted to turn back time. I stepped up the effort even more with the third. No better, maybe worse. I had one more chance, all out blitz in his final year. When I dropped him off I discovered the civil war in my head and heart had gone nuclear. This was not fair.

Over and over I kept thinking, "C'mon. What more could I have done?" The answer finally broke through: nothing. There simply are not enough hugs. It was not lack of effort, it is a reality that I hate living with and can no longer deny. Distance and separation hurt. *Bad!*

It is not possible to fill up our hearts to ward off the heartbreak.

There just simply are not enough hugs.

No matter how many times, we will always wish for one more hug. No matter how many times we embrace, verbalize our love, share good times, our hearts will break when we have to say good-bye.

It is not something I did or didn't do; it is the reality of life that doesn't make any sense to our heads. There is nothing that can keep us from longing for those we love.

And it is not just hugs. You can substitute the word "hugs" with all the other things we enjoy. Smiles, dinners, walks, ballgames, concerts, touches, laughs, and on and on and on and on and on... We think, "Just one more..." Take it from a dad who kept giving "just one more" – doesn't work. There just aren't enough to fill our hearts.

There are always regrets. In truth, it is impossible to do everything we wanted to do because it would have taken 60 years of 48-hour days. There just isn't enough time or resources. So choices are made, and our faulty best really is enough.

Hence, the empty nest is here. An era is over. It is right. It is good. It is as it should be. It just stinks that my heart can hurt this bad when things are going the way they should!!! But I've realized that if I let myself bawl and grieve it, the memories get brighter, stronger and more meaningful as the loss fades. Grieving allows me to let go in a healthy way, develop an even stronger, healthier relationship with these adults that look an awful lot like the little kids that used to run around our house.

But there is coming a day

Perhaps God allows us to long for more in our relationships so that we are not satisfied with the here and now. Could it be true that if we found total contentment in this life we would be settling for a poor facsimile? Whether intended or not, the longing for more time, more hugs, more moments is what turns our eyes to eternity. There we will not long for more; we will, for the first time, be completely satisfied. Until then, let's love and live.

> And I heard a loud voice from the throne saying, "Behold, the dwelling place of God is with man. He will dwell with them, and they will be his people, and God himself will be with them as their God. He will wipe away every tear from their eyes, and death shall be no more, neither shall there be mourning, nor crying, nor pain anymore, for the former things have passed away."
> -- Revelation 21:3–4 (ESV)

> For his anger is but for a moment, and his favor is for a lifetime. Weeping may tarry for the night, but joy comes with the morning.
> -- Psalm 30:5

Part Eight: Never Ending, Ever Changing

CHAPTER THIRTY-FIVE

GOD AND I HAD A FIGHT

To sit on God's lap leads us to be used by God

God and I had a fight a while back. Didn't mean to. Didn't want to. It wasn't a knock-down, drag out affair. I mean, c'mon, really. When has that even been possible with God? Old Testament Jacob tried it and limped away with a permanent hip injury. You might get knocked down and drug out, but God won't break a sweat.

I actually didn't even *want* to fight with God, it's just that, well, sometimes God asks some pretty awkward stuff. Stuff that looks like it's going to get embarrassing.

Chadd, my youngest son, and I joined a bunch of other Keystone Oaks Marching Band parents to set up the Christmas tree sale. Unloading over 900 trees is a great time of working together. After six hours, the final clean up was winding down when Tom, another parent, and I started talking.

"How are you doing?" I asked Tom, employing standard conversation starter language. Instead of the usual, "Fine," he actually told me the truth - he hurt his neck a couple days before and was in excruciating pain. It got so bad the previous day that he had gone to the emergency room. Even the elephant sized pain killers he brought home weren't helping much and he had been awake since 2:00 am.

This was when God and I got into it. Loud and clear I got the message from God that I should pray for Tom. You might know that kind of impression. There are times when "a good idea" comes to mind. Sometimes it is and sometimes it isn't. Those thoughts are usually common sense, or my thoughts. On the other end of the spectrum, there are times when a thought pops into my mind and it is not just a good idea, it is a GOD idea. Strong, definite, significant, no option orders. I've learned these are something that I had better do. That it is not about me but what God is up to and giving me the honor to be part of it.

"Okay, God. I'm willing, but there are a lot of people around and I don't want to embarrass Tom."

Sounds so kind and spiritual, doesn't it? I could almost hear God making chicken squawking noises at me.

"Pray for Tom."

"Okay, God. I'm not saying 'No' here; I just want to do this properly." (Which is good sometimes, but I've also learned that God is not overly concerned with "proper." Just ask Mary and Joseph.)

"Pray for Tom."

I walked away. I wasn't trying to get out of it, just making sure it was really God and not me. Really.

People began to leave, Chadd and I stayed to make sure everything was cleaned up, to make sure Tom didn't lift anything and to look for an opportunity. Problem was, another guy that didn't seem like the praying kind, kept hanging around to help Tom as well. Didn't want to shirk, didn't want to embarrass. The guys just kept hanging around.

So I did the spiritual, pastor thing. I left. I know, I know. I wasn't really running, I had just gotten myself so worked up that I was doubting my ability to hear God. Why do we make these things so hard? As we drove away, the voice in my head refused to shut up.

"Pray for Tom."

I turned around at the next street. "Dad, what are you doing?"

"I think I'm supposed to pray for Tom."

"Okay." Chadd was readier than I was.

We drove back to the parking lot where Tom, his wife, his son and the other dad were still talking at a picnic table. I promptly drove right past.

"Pray for Tom."

Not mean, not loud, but ever so clear and distinct. This was not me, this was God. And there was no way He was letting this go. The only way to get out of this was to blatantly, intentionally refuse. Which brings us to another lesson I've learned: If I choose to refuse, I take a step away from closeness with God. That hurts me and, I've found, it hurts other people. I certainly didn't want to step away from God. Been there, done that and it ain't pretty. It was becoming increasingly obvious that God wanted to do something for Tom, and this was not about me. I certainly did not want to rob him of God's touch. I've been in pain and I don't want anyone to endure it a second longer than necessary.

Part Eight: Never Ending, Ever Changing

Besides that, now my son knew what God wanted me to do, so there was another layer of stuff going on.

"PRAY. FOR. TOM!"

We went through the intersection and turned left – the way home. Chadd probably thought I'd lost my ever lovin' mind. "How many times are we going to drive by before you just do this?" he could have asked, but didn't. Turned around at the next intersection and headed back to the now familiar parking lot. Yep, the whole crew was still there.

With God watching, and Chadd wondering, I finally had the courage to turn into the parking lot, drive up to the group, get out and walk toward them. They all grinned and teased. "What did you forget?"

"Nothing. Just returning the screw you gave me," I said to the other parent and held out my hand. He smiled, remembering he had given me the gift of a bent screw while working together. Christmas spirit, you know.

Deep breath. (And you thought us pastors had it all together). "Actually, I feel like I'm supposed to pray for you, Tom. Would that be alright?"

"Sure. Every little bit helps," he agreed gladly. This would have been easy if I'd obeyed as soon as I got the message.

"Well, I'll be going home now," said the other parent. I told you he didn't like the praying kind. He left, I put my hand on Tom's shoulder and prayed. Nothing profound, simply that God would remove the pain, heal the source of the problem and let Tom do the things he wants to do. No sparks. Frankly, I felt nothing at all. Sometimes, I sense the Presence of God, but this time I felt nothing except relief that I obeyed. We talked for a few more minutes. Tom and his wife appreciated the concern and mentioned again how every little bit helps.

And we went home, very glad that I obeyed, as much for myself as for Tom. That was Saturday. The following week Tom came to mind, I wondered how he was doing and I continued to pray for him.

Friday evening rolled around. "Oh, Dad," Chadd said, "I saw Tom at the tree sale Tuesday night. I'm sorry I should have told you sooner. He said to tell you that when he woke up Sunday morning the pain was completely gone."

All I could do was stare at the boy. ***Wow!*** God actually healed Tom just that quick. Excruciating pain that doctors and drugs could not touch. Gone. ***Gone!***

I nearly shook with the sobering realization of how close I had come to disobeying God, harming Tom and missing the privilege God was giving me to be used for something quite significant.

I almost allowed Tom to continue in harsh agony when our loving Heavenly Dad wanted to release His power and Tom's pain. To think I almost let some immature fear of embarrassment get in the way of a true miracle.

After I stopped kicking myself, my spirit soared the rest of the evening. *This is what makes life interesting, fulfilling and worth living!*

I have ***got*** to stop fighting with God.

> If we live by the Spirit, let us also keep in step with the Spirit.
> -- Galatians 5:25

> Now to him who is able to do far more abundantly than all that we ask or think, according to the power at work within us, to him be glory in the church and in Christ Jesus throughout all generations, forever and ever. Amen.
> -- Ephesians 3:20–21

Part Eight: Never Ending, Ever Changing

CHAPTER THIRTY-SIX

WHEN JESUS WAS STRONGEST

To sit on God's lap leads us to strength when it seems we should be weak

Counter-intuitive.

I was wrong! I can't believe that I was wrong about this. It seemed like common sense, a no-brainer. But I was wrong. Though I've read the account a hundred times and thought I had it right, I was wrong.

Lying in bed, just before going to sleep, I grabbed the Bible by my bed and read Matthew 4. It is the account of Jesus in the desert for forty days with no food and no human companions, when He goes toe to toe with the devil. At the end of the forty days, the Bible states, "he (Jesus) was hungry." I used to consider that one of the great understatements, but I've learned that feelings of hunger disappear during an extended fast, reappearing only when the body has no more reserves and needs to eat to prevent damage.

It was at that point of no reserves that the devil ramped up the temptations, coming after Jesus with the big three: turn rocks into bread, jump off the temple, and bow to the devil to sidestep the pain.

I correctly understood the scripture to that point. But I was wrong concerning a very important truth about Jesus' condition. I always thought and taught that, at the end of the forty days, Jesus was at His weakest and thus most vulnerable when the devil came after Him hard. As I read the passage this time, God popped a new understanding into my head.

Note: there are times when thoughts come to mind that are not ours. Different than normal, wiser, more insightful and that resonate in the soul as well as the mind. That is the Holy Spirit privileging us with His insights. That is "revelation." We are not that smart. So breathe a prayer of thanks and give God credit when you tell others.

Back to Matthew 4. Here's the insight – Jesus was not at His weakest but at His *strongest*! Though I held the exact opposite belief for decades, in that moment, I knew it was true. It suddenly made complete sense. I was amazed.

It is true that Jesus was worn out from forty days without nourishment and fighting off the devil. But, because He had spent forty uninterrupted, undistracted, uniquely focused days with the Father through the counter-intuitive discipline of fasting and prayer, Jesus was the *strongest* He had ever been. Scripture confirms it…

> And when the devil had ended every temptation, he departed from him until an opportune time. And Jesus returned in the power of the Spirit to Galilee, and a report about him went out through all the surrounding country.   -- Luke 4:13–14

Soooooo… Is it possible God might be calling you and me to pray and fast regularly to fill us with the same strength? Is it possible that an extended time denying ourselves food and setting aside time to be with God might result in being the *strongest* we've ever been?

It really makes no sense. It is counter-intuitive, contrary to common sense expectations. We expect that we would get weak, and physically there is truth to that. But spiritually, emotionally and mentally, fasting and prayer leads to *strength.*

Let's be candid and not Pollyanna naïve. It is hard. Even with God's help, it is hard. But hard is not bad. Hard is just hard and this kind of hard leads to good.

It is counter-intuitive to healthy living in the physical realm, but in the spiritual realm, it is *the* right formula for experiencing God.

Fasting empowered prayer is a ***path to deeper intimacy with Loving Heavenly Dad*** not a harsh command by a demanding, harsh authoritarian.

Fasting fueled prayer is one of the most powerful ways to crawl on to God's lap. God's first invitation to do so came to me after two consecutive Tuesday through Thursday fasts. That was not coincidence.

Which brings us to an important decision.

Choice One: Take the hard road of discipline. That path means saying "no" to food to say "yes" to God. It means experiencing God's promise that the Holy Spirit's power will work supernaturally in our lives and with those we love. This path means gaining the ability to hear God more clearly, to live more confidently, to experience greater satisfaction, and to crawl up on His lap more often.

Part Eight: Never Ending, Ever Changing

– OR –

Choice Two: Take the path that seems easier. This path means saying "yes" to your desires and "no" to God. It means refusing all He longs to do in you and for you. It means turning away from so much of what we really want (but don't realize it) and experiencing *way, way, way* less than God wants for you.

Your choice.

EPILOGUE

The Joy We Get, The Joy We Give

THE JOY WE GET, THE JOY WE GIVE

To <u>sit on God's lap brings unimaginable joy to Him and to us</u>

We recently flew from Pittsburgh to Seattle for a family wedding. Sheila, me, our daughter Carissa, and most important of all, our grandson, Brodie. Fourteen month-old Brodie, who, as previously mentioned, is non-stop boy. He has two speeds: full ahead and sleep. We approached the airplane ride with a lot of question marks. Seattle is the geographically farthest spot from Pittsburgh in the lower forty-eight of the United States. Translated, that means a looooong flight when traveling with a fourteen month-old boy. Did I mention he is all boy?

One can choose a positive attitude or a negative attitude when approaching such a situation. With dread or excitement. As a problem or an opportunity. Expecting it to be bad or anticipating it to be good. We chose excitement, opportunity and good. Carissa did a tremendous job of stocking her carry on with food and toys. I stocked up on prayer. The flight to Seattle was uneventful. The toddler ate, played and slept. I was so happy.

Two events happened over the rest of the trip that reminded me again of our loving Heavenly Dad's care for us.

A sick boy and a happy grandpa

First, Brodie came down with a bad cold the second day in Seattle. The little guy was miserable. His throat hurt. His head hurt. His joints ached. He couldn't breathe well, which meant he couldn't sleep well. The apartment where the four of us were staying became a sick room. We rotated the care for Brodie, taking turns sleeping, holding him, making meals and making medicine runs.

After several days, Carissa was worn out as Brodie fussed instead of sleeping, wanting to be held through the night. I got up somewhere around 2:00 a.m. to give her relief. Understand, I am old. Because I am old, I no longer do late night well. It takes me years to recover from a late night, let alone a middle of the night shift. But I did it to help my daughter.

Carissa wearily put Brodie into my arms as I made myself comfortable in an easy chair. As she walked away, Brodie nestled his little head into my chest and put his arms around me. Suddenly my grogginess was gone as his chest rose and fell with each breath and I felt the warmth of his little body against mine. Rather than being frustrated that he was sick, I guiltily found myself glad. When healthy, he doesn't slow down long enough to be held long, but here, in the middle of the night, I had the incredible privilege of holding him on my lap for hours. Those hours filled my heart. When he awoke, we shared some cookies and milk on my lap. Another rare, precious moment.

Carissa returned hours later, apologizing for sleeping so long. Silly girl. I tried to convince her that it was a privilege, a true honor to hold Brodie as he slept. I'm not sure she believed me as I tried to convince her that losing sleep with a sick child was nothing compared to the joy, the sacred moments that occurred in the darkest hours of the night.

But it was. And still is. And is so with God.

In those hours, I caught a glimpse of God.

I think it is difficult to transfer our focus from ourselves to God. To grasp that our Heavenly Dad feels emotions. That we, as His children, bring joy or heartache to Him just as our children do with us. We get so caught up in what we are experiencing and do not understand that God's call to His lap is not a command to force us to do something we'd rather not, but rather an invitation for both God and us to experience the kind of joy that surprised me as I held Brodie.

I'm not glad Brodie got sick. I am glad that I could be there when he was. Sickness, rather than ruining a vacation, opened the door for Brodie to experience the love his grandpa has for him. And opened my heart to experience the joy of holding a dearly loved child.

As it is with God. Is it possible that God allows us to be sick or tired or hurting or disappointed (He could change any of it, after all) so that we and He will experience something deeper, something more satisfying, when we crawl up on His lap?

A scared boy and a fearless grandpa

Weary from the week and sad to leave our family in Seattle, we boarded the plane for the trip home. Brodie was well and at full tilt again.

Epilogue: The Joy We Get, The Joy We Give

The airplane, amazingly, was not full on the final leg from Chicago to Pittsburgh that Tuesday evening. Carissa took a window seat, I took the aisle and put Brodie in the middle. Grandma was banished to a seat across the aisle.

"We will not be serving drinks due to turbulence," came the announcement.

"That can't be good," I thought. I've flown enough to know Southwest cancels concessions rarely and only with good reason.

We experienced some bumpiness during the first half of the flight, but Brodie was able to stand on the middle seat with little trouble.

"All passengers must now return to their seats and buckle securely. Traffic control tells us we are headed into some strong pockets of unstable air." Perhaps they should provide counseling for the air and it wouldn't be so unstable. Yeah, you're right. It's doesn't help many of the people either.

Then the first unstable air hit us. Hard. Carissa had Brodie on her lap and terror in her eyes. She's not flown much and was not having fun.

"It's going to be okay," I said as another pocket dropped the plane a few feet, imitating a roller coaster. My words were trumped by the roiling in Carissa's stomach.

Another unstable bit of air and Carissa's eyes went from saucers to dinner plates.

"Let me hold Brodie," I offered, to which she handed him over quickly.

I don't know how scared he was, but he was not happy with being tossed back and forth by the movement of the plane. So I held him tight.

I glanced to Sheila's seat of banishment to see her face an odd shade of green and leaning forward. Carissa saw her, too.

"Pray, Dad! Pray, cause I'm really scared."

I don't claim to be overly brave, but I've been through enough of these rough rides to know that it is part of flying and nothing to be concerned about. In fact, the whole thing made me smile and chuckle.

Apparently that wasn't helpful to Carissa.

"Pray, Dad. Right now!" So I did. And the plane kept bucking.

Brodie wanted to go back to the middle seat. So I held him tighter as the plane pitched again. Then he did get scared. Started fussing and struggling. Just like we do with God sometimes. When He needs to hold us tightest we seem to fight Him the most. Out of fear, or discomfort, or the strangeness of what is happening. And no amount of assurances will cause us to settle.

As the planed dipped, rose, and jerked from side to side I held the boy tighter than I ever have before. I whispered to him (and reassured his mom). "Ssshhh. It's okay," but it didn't seem to help. I held him tighter as he struggled more.

So I sang. In the midst of the jostling, I sang songs familiar to Brodie. Songs that usually settle him, that bring a smile, that bring him comfort. He settled for a bit, but would struggle again as the plane lurched. Held him tighter and sang some more.

Settle, lurch, struggle, sing, snug him closer.

Settle, lurch, struggle, sing, snug him closer.

All the way to the ground.

Sheila started losing the green hue. Carissa breathed a sigh of relief. Brodie relaxed as I put him in the middle seat. All was right again.

In those hours, I caught another glimpse of God.

Carissa apologized for being afraid and not holding on to Brodie. I'm not sure she believed me as I tried to convince her that holding tight and singing to the boy was a privilege and a joy. That I experienced a deep satisfaction that I could hold, protect, reassure and keep Brodie safe. That those short minutes had been a unique kind of sacred moment.

But it was. And still is. And is so with God

Just when we need God to hold us tightest, we seem to fight Him the most. Out of fear, or discomfort, or the strangeness of what is happening. And no amount of assurances will cause us to settle. But He doesn't scold us or tell us not to be afraid. He holds us tighter, and if we listen closely, we can hear Him singing to us as He holds us as tight as necessary to get us through life's turbulence safely.

It's time. Let God be your loving Heavenly Dad. Give Him more joy than you can imagine as you crawl into His lap to find all you long for.

ABOUT THE AUTHOR

Herb Shaffer has over 35 years of experience as a leader, teacher, pastor, trainer, mentor, and motivational speaker. He is currently pastor of New Song Community Church, a church he founded in 1991, which is located in the south suburbs of Pittsburgh, PA. He also serves as Director of the Institute for Servant Leadership, an organization that "exists to equip Christians to be effective servant leaders in the local church."

Herb's life was transformed by God through the people of Maiden Lane Church of God in Springfield, Ohio, his hometown. He has made it his mission to do the same for others in any way possible.

Herb graduated with a Bachelor's degree in Pastoral Ministry and Bible from Gulf-Coast Bible College, (now Mid-America Christian University) in 1981, and received a Master's of Science in Organizational Leadership degree from Geneva College, Beaver Falls, PA in 2001. He is a trained, certified teacher and coach in communication with Dynamic Communications International, led by Ken Davis.

Herb has taught college courses in leadership, organizational dynamics, critical thinking, communication, and life development, has written curriculum for Warner Press and has been published in several Christian magazines.

Intimacy and Awe: Walking with the Real God is Herb Shaffer's second published book. He also authored *From Where God Sits: A Quest to Discover God's Perspective*, (2014).

Herb and his wife, Sheila, are the proud parents of four adult children and grandparents of five.

ACKNOWLEDGMENTS

One of my favorite films ends with every-man George Bailey reading a note from the angel who rescued him. "Dear George, remember, no man is a failure who has friends. Thanks for the wings. Love, Clarence."[13] Director Frank Capra said that he wanted to create it to be *"A film that said to the downtrodden, the pushed-around, the pauper, 'Head's up, fella. No man is poor who has one friend. Three friends and you're filthy rich.'"*[14]

I am amazed at how blessed I am with family and friends. Frank Capra is right, true wealth is not measured by bank accounts, but by friendships. I am a successful, filthy rich man! Thank you to all who consider me a friend. Specifically (and inadequately) my gratitude goes the people below who helped bring this book to print.

… Kelly Opferman. You believed in this book and went above and beyond in giving your time, expertise and love to make it a reality. Never could I sufficiently express my thanks for the many hours you gave to keep me from grammatical suicide and tweaking my words to convey what was in my heart. You have no idea how much value you have added!

… Amber Bethel. Your ability to see what I do not see and use your artistic ability to create pictures that come alive is extraordinary. Thank you for finding the picture and creating the cover that draws people to the book. I love you, my daughter.

… Michael Matti. Though we've never met, you allowed me to use the cover photo captures the theme of intimacy and awe in a remarkable way.

…the people of the congregations who allowed me to serve as pastor and grew with me. You encouraged, supported, prayed and loved our family through the journey this book describes: Cardiff Road Church of God; Maple Grove Church of God; Beaver Valley Church of God; New Song Community Church.

… my children, Andrew, Carissa, Amber, and Chadd who God has used to show me God's intimacy and awe through our experiences together. It is an honor to be your dad. I am proud of you. Thanks, too, for giving me grandchildren to keep the picture of intimacy fresh.

… my wife, Sheila, who has put up with my quirks and humor for lo, these many years. Thank you for patiently enduring all the hours I was buried in this book. I love you.

… first and most of all, God, who, all my life has pursued me as a Loving Heavenly Dad and revealed Himself as Holy, Almighty God. I love sitting on Your lap and bowing at Your feet. There is no greater joy. Thank you for all You are and all You do. Words can never express my love and gratitude. Ever.   Herb Shaffer, May 2018

[1] Magic Eye® images are a product of Magic Eye Inc., PO Box 1986, Provincetown, MA 02657
[2] Chip Ingram used this exercise when he spoke at the February 4, 2017 No Regrets men's conference.
[3] *Tozer, A.W., "Knowledge of Holy", Harper Collins, 1961.*
[4] https://www.si.com/si-kids/photo/2016/10/25/professional-athletes-and-their-kids
[5] *Batterson, Mark, Wild Goose Chase. Multnomah Publishing, 2008. p. 108*
[6] *Collins, Ace, "Stories Behind the Best Loved Songs of Christmas", pages 53--57, Zondervan Publishing, 2001.*
[7] The Princess Bride, 20th Century Fox, 1987.
[8] *Eldredge, John, Waking the Dead. Thomas Nelson, 2003.*
[9] The SCORRE© Conference, a division of Dynamic Communicators, Inc., 105 SE Parkway, Ste 107, Franklin, TN 37064. http://www.scorreconference.tv/
[10] *Alcorn, Randy, The Treasure Principle, Multnomah Books, 2001*
[11] http://mathworld.wolfram.com/Line.html
[12] *Alcorn, Randy, The Treasure Principle, Multnomah Books, 2001*
[13] Capra, F., Stewart, J., & Liberty Films. (1946). *It's a wonderful life.* Los Angeles, CA: Liberty Films.
[14] http://www.marintheatre.org/productions/wonderful-life/iawl-the-name-above-the-title-an-excerpt